UGLY

The Aesthetics
Of Everything

Stephen Bayley

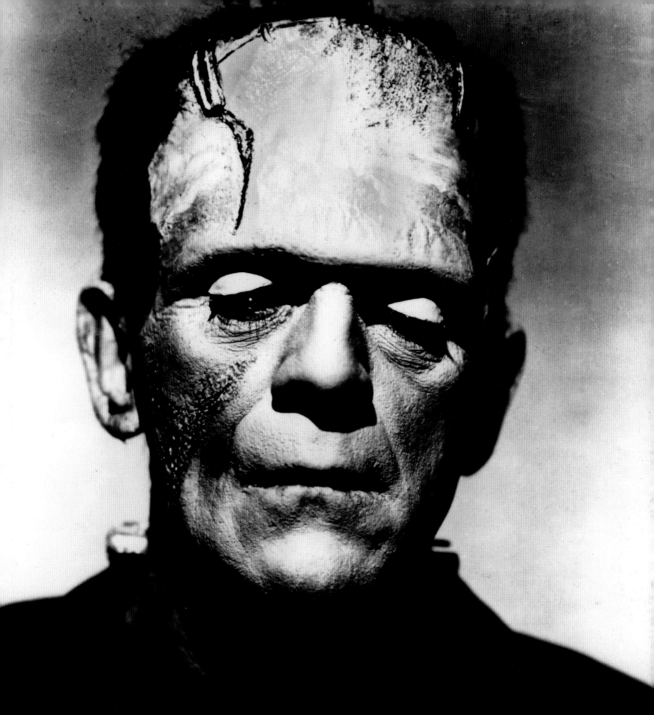

UGLY

The Aesthetics
Of Everything

Stephen Bayley

The Overlook Press
New York, NY

Page 2 The philosopher Edmund Burke undermined the functionalist theory of beauty. He said if we truly valued the way things work, the efficient pig would be considered beautiful.

Page 3 Boris Karloff in *Frankenstein* (1931). The actor was as much a fiction as Dr Frankenstein's monster. "Boris Karloff" was an invention of the English actor William Henry Pratt. To play Mary Shelley's stumbling monster he wore four inch platform shoes weighing thirteen pounds, creating the signature monstrous lurch.

Page 4–5 The terrible beauty of weapons: Maverick and Sidewinder missiles being loaded onto an A-10 "Warthog" in Gulf War 1. Ugly functional requirements often give military equipment a harrowing elegance. The aeroplane was thus named due to its extremely ugly aspect.

Page 6 By many standards, the bulldog is deformed. A prognathous jaw, folds of limp flesh, bowed legs and crushed features all challenge conventions of canine elegance. Yet the bulldog is both a symbol representative of Britain, and a mascot for the US Marine Corps.

This edition first published in hardcover in the United States in 2013 by The Overlook Press, Peter Mayer Publishers, Inc.
141 Wooster Street
New York, NY 10012
www.overlookpress.com
For bulk and special sales please contact sales@overlookny.com
or write us at the above address

Text © 2012 Stephen Bayley

Design © 2012 Goodman Fiell

Cataloging-in-Publication data is available from the Library of Congress

Publishing Directors: Charlotte & Peter Fiell

Project Editor: Isabel Wilkinson

Editorial: Rosanna Negrotti and Barry Goodman

Picture Sourcing: Steve Behan, Charlotte Fiell, Ben White and Isabel Wilkinson

Design: Peter Dawson and Louise Evans, www.gradedesign.com

Cover Design: Grade Design and Mark Thomson

Indexing: Lesley Malkin

Production Manager: Maria Petalidou

Printed in China

ISBN 978-1-4683-0716-0

Contents

A NOTE ON THE TEXT, as they often write in books more pompous than this one is intended to be.

Why did I want to write *Ugly*? Well, one answer is as follows. For as long as I can remember, I have been helplessly engrossed with the look of things, whether a ketchup bottle or a temple, a woman or a car. Amateur and indeed professional Freudians might attribute so near an obsession with shapes and surfaces to some traumatic childhood event best left deeply repressed. Or, less charitably, it may be attributed to a crude infatuation with superficialities and effects: a pimp writes on love, say. Still, as Pedro Almodóvar once said, if it's not autobiography, it's plagiarism.

But I hope it's more interesting than that. I care passionately about appearances and I have always wanted to understand them. So the astringent P. J. O'Rourke has a nice put-down for someone like me who worries about what cars, for instance, mean. O'Rourke says, "Cars mean you don't have to walk home". But while O'Rourke and I are, I'm guessing, at one with Voltaire's quip that it's *mieux perdre un ami, qu'un bon mot*, there's more to ugliness than just a few smart gags. The construct of beauty versus ugliness is one of the most perplexing in our imaginations. Is there actually such a thing as ugliness? It's commonplace to assume the answer is yes.

And it's equally commonplace to assume that ugliness is necessarily bad; for Albert Camus, to offer one absurd example, it was beauty that he found unbearable:

"[Beauty] drives us to despair, offering for a minute the glimpse of an eternity that we should like to stretch out over the whole of time."

So beauty is unattainable, while ugliness is unavoidable? Maybe beauty excites metaphysical speculation, while ugliness merely makes us annoyed. And "beauty" is not always satisfying. Beautiful perfection can be boring and sometimes downright disturbing. In the worlds of robotics and computer-generated imagery there is a phenomenon known as the "uncanny valley", which explains why when robots begin closely to approximate human appearance and when computer-generated characters become increasingly photo-realistic they can possess an uncomfortable eeriness to them – essentially, too perfect to be human. Famously in *Final Fantasy: The Spirits Within* (2001) – the first CGI (computer-generated image) film featuring synthetic human actors – the characters were generally found to be too disquietingly perfect with their chillingly regular features, and as a result the movie bombed. Interestingly, 3D animators are now taught to design-in imperfections, so that their characters are more realistically human, warts and all, and thereby more pleasing.

It is easy to make the claim that ugliness is not the opposite of beauty, but one aspect of it. Plato describes the queasy fascination of a pile of corpses beneath an executioner's dais: similarly, we cannot drag our eyes off accidents and atrocities.

Opposite David Moratilla, *Close Up Portrait*, 2011. Small flaws often enhance beautiful features. This digital image was created to suggest compromised perfection, and to counteract the 'uncanny valley' effect.

But you can't write a historical narrative on ugliness, at least not in the academic sense. The books simply do not exist: appropriate to its aggressive nature, ugliness is a subject writers have generally avoided. Perhaps they have avoided it like a plague.

Of course, there are the great philosophical works which treat with beauty – but I am not going to pretend to have read, still less understood, Plato and Kant. True, in his 1970 posthumously-published masterpiece *Ästhetische Theorie*, the noted, but incomprehensible, critic Theodor Adorno has some long, vague passages on ugliness where he says, 'In the ugly, art must denounce the world.' But I am also not going to pretend I understand Adorno.

So this establishes some useful distance between *Ugly* and other works of pop aesthetics: many of Plato's ideas have slipped into popular thought, but I don't believe that most of the people who quote from Kant's *Kritik der reinen Vernunft* (1781) have actually read it. Certainly, I have not. But then, nor do I quote from it. Anyway, if you want to read about the amphiboly of concepts of reflection, I'm afraid you're in the wrong book.

And when modern authors have confronted ugliness, as Karl Rosenkranz once did and Umberto Eco did recently, the results are mixed. Rosenkranz, whose *Ästhetik des Häßlichen* was published in German in 1853 and, so far as I can tell, has never troubled a translator, was a follower of Hegel and therefore probably too baffling for most of us. Eco's *Storia della Bruttezza* is altogether more accessible, especially as an English edition titled *On Ugliness* was published in 2007. Like everything with Eco's name on it – he is the "curator" rather than the author of the book – *Bruttezza* is wonderfully evocative and ruminative, but nowhere in it does he truly confront the subject in hand. The book's a fascinating account of grotesques, freaks and devils. Not quite the same thing as ugliness.

I'm not much inclined to paddle in the pools of relativism, but the more you think about ugliness, the more you look at ugliness, the more elusive the idea becomes. Aesthetics is the science of beauty, but it's an imprecise science. In fact, in terms of evidence and repeatable experimental results and peer review, it's not a science at all.

I hope when you look and read *Ugly* you'll begin to wonder exactly why we prefer the Boboli Gardens to the hellscape of Gehenna, or just why and how did the 1954 Glöckler Porsche come to be so hideous. Who can explain why Quentin Massys' *Ugly Duchess* is one of the most popular pictures in London's National Gallery? If there are rules, they are flexible ones. But there is one rule that isn't: look at everything, think about it and wonder… at the meaning of it all. And then reflect on Kenneth Tynan's brief to himself: "Rouse tempers, goad and lacerate, raise whirlwinds!"

BELVEDE

ON PITTI

1. Perfection, or No Dirt and Mess in Heaven

Is it natural to be disgusted?
Exactly what attracts and repels us?
Why are slums unpleasant?
Is Heaven neat and tidy?
Is beauty simple or complex?
Do distress and deformity inspire art?

We need to start with something disgusting.

It is one of the most startling "discoveries" of nineteenth-century science that responses to disgusting stimuli are not entirely arbitrary, but predictable and measurable. This was an important part of Charles Darwin's later research as he moved on from the grandiosity of evolutionary theory to the particularities of human and animal behaviour. I have put "discoveries" in inverted commas because scientific results, perhaps at least as much as artistic achievements, are a product of contemporary taste, driven by momentary appetites rather than eternal verities.

But while Darwin did indeed determine that similar facial expressions might be employed by people from different cultures, the stimulus that might cause a disgusted facial expression is different in, say, Lapland from Belgravia. In his book *The Origin of Food Habits* (1944) H. D. Renner describes one tribe that takes positive pleasure in rotten fish. And rotten fish, in a concoction known as *garum,* was a staple of Roman cooking. Made from the intestines of small fish, macerated in salt and sun-dried, garum also had a depilatory effect. In the United States it would be illegal…and disgusting.

Before Darwin identified the universality of what's disgusting by analyzing facial responses, it had been considered by Leonardo da Vinci. The way to perfection, Leonardo believed, is "through a series of disgusts". This expression we owe to Walter Pater, the Victorian essayist whose thoughts on the Mona Lisa have passed into collective consciousness. Pater argued that Leonardo's version of beauty was rooted more in fascination than in delight. He was not searching for beauty – he was searching for information. And this led him to an unbiased treatment of ugliness.

In his notebooks Leonardo describes his disgust at the idea of heterosexual intercourse; as a result of this, his anatomical drawings of women are belligerently un-erotic. So far from making a naked woman a source of aesthetic pleasure, Leonardo prefers to make her disgusting. Or ugly. Just a lot of cloacal plumbing and gaping orifices.

Leonardo also had a more general interest in ugliness. His drawings betray a fascination with deformity and disfigurement. In fact, for many centuries Leonardo's work was better known through copies of these troubling drawings than through his solemnly beautiful paintings. You could say that there was a Leonardo da Vinci ugliness industry. So much so

1

2

3

4

5

6

Left and previous In *The Expression of the Emotions in Man and Animals* (1872) Charles Darwin proposed that facial expressions are consistently revealing of emotions. He proposed also that some have a practical basis: the gesture of affirmation or negation, a nod or a shake of the head, is based on a child's acceptance or refusal of the mother's nipple. And in response to any disgusting stimulus, a predictable set of facial gestures occurs. Instinctively, Darwin says, people protect their faces from aggressive, or ugly, stimuli. Left is an illustration from the book using photographs by Duchenne du Boulogne, whose work on physiognomy greatly inspired Darwin: "Joy, High Spirits, Love, Tender Feelings, Devotion". Previous page:"Cat terrified by a dog".

Overleaf Leonardo da Vinci's Mona Lisa, oil on poplar (c.1503–1506). The enigmatic *La Gioconda*, "The Smiling One", defies interpretation, but indisputably represents one ideal of female beauty. Yet Leonardo was as interested in freaks as in perfection. His fascination with "Grotesque Heads", as shown in this sketch (c.1490), is evidence of his turbulent imagination and questing intelligence. So far as his notebooks are concerned, Leonardo was as interested in human ugliness as human beauty.

that the very existence of his grotesque drawings perplexed the great art historians and Leonardo experts Kenneth Clark and E. H. Gombrich. In his 1952 lectures on the Grotesque Heads Gombrich said, "In what might be called the pre-humanitarian age such monstrosities and malformations – the dwarf, the cripple and the bizarre physiognomy – belonged to the category of 'curiosities' to be gaped at". Maybe, but to Leonardo, you could not have a meaningful *bellezza* without an equally meaningful *bruttezza*.

The everlasting din of machinery

The idea that disgusting experiences can create an appetite for perfection is an important one: ugliness demands redress by beauty. It was through a series of very nasty, vivid and dirty "disgusts" that one of the most curious and moving experiments in artistic – if not social – perfection was achieved. This was the Shakers, an American utopian community that had its origins in the Manchester of the Industrial Revolution.

How disgusting Manchester might have been in the late eighteenth century may be gauged from how very disgusting it most certainly was in

Above left/right Manchester's docks in 1883 and its Union Street in 1835. The city's industrial culture made disturbing impressions: the squalor drove Ann Lee to America where, in an inspired state of denial, she founded the Shakers. The same conditions made the Romantic Robert Southey moan about the 'everlasting din of machinery' and inspired Friedrich Engels to political action. But the very same factories inspired the architect Karl Friedrich Schinkel, whose austere classicism predicted Modernism.

COTTON FACTORIES, UNION STREET, MANCHESTER.

the early 19th when local lad, Friedrich Engels, wrote his *Conditions of the Working Class in England* (1844), based on his eyewitness experiences on the streets of Ancoats and Chorlton-on-Medlock. The engines of the Industrial Revolution, at least in this part of the world, were the cotton mills, and they sucked in humans as fuel with as much pitiless efficiency as they spewed out filth.

Land was expensive and conditions infernal. There was, of course, no lighting apart from tallow candles, no ventilation and no sanitation. A family of ten might live in a single room no more than 100 feet square. A report of 1832 described one area where a single lavatory was used by 380 people. In nearby Liverpool, it was estimated that 10 per cent of the population actually lived underground in cellars where sewage seeped in. Cholera was endemic.

Jonathan Aitken described a Manchester where there were anarchic dunghills on the muddy roads that were, of course, not yet covered with Macadam's controlling synthetic surface. Beds were infested and a hot bath cost the equivalent of £11. When he visited Manchester in 1808, Robert Southey said "a place more destitute of all interesting objects… is not easy to conceive." And he continued to describe the teeming population:

"Imagine this multitude crowded together in narrow streets, the homes all built of brick and blackened with smoke; frequent buildings among them as large as convents, without their antiquity, without their beauty, without their holiness; where you hear from within… the everlasting din of machinery; and where, when the bell rings, it is to call the wretches to their work instead of their prayers."

In summary, Manchester was ugly. And it was this disgusting experience that stimulated one of the most poignant acts of escapism. From this diseased squalor, a poor girl of the serving classes called Ann Lee contrived her physical, metaphysical and spiritual escape. Already in touch with the Quakers, the illiterate – but evidently charismatic – Lee melded escape, piety and vision into a new way of life in dramatic contrast to the ugliness she grew up with. Imprisoned for breaking the Sabbath, she had the first of her miraculous visions.

The miracle of her visions was matched in intensity only by her determination to reinvent her identity and her world. Leaving Manchester, Ann Lee arrived in New York State aged 38 on 6 August 1774, and established herself and her followers near present-day Watervliet. She established the United Society of Believers in Christ's Second Appearing and, declaring "there is no dirt in heaven," Mother Lee (as she soon became known) decided to create in New Lebanon the ideal community that her native Lancashire so evidently lacked. In a telling gesture, sex was abandoned in favour of ecstatic communal dancing.

On account of the paroxysms her ecstatic dancers experienced, her Society became – at first derisively – known as the Shakers. Mother Lee's Shakers developed a work ethic of formidable and unhesitating perfectionism: celibacy, industry, purity and a unique aesthetic became one. It found expression in utilitarian buildings, furniture and generalised asceticism

Above Shakers near Mount
Lebanon, New York (circa 1870).
The entire Shaker civilization
repudiated urban, industrial culture.
Their ecstatic gatherings produced
the voluptuous, rhythmic bodily
movements that inspired their
name. Shakers also repudiated sex
and enlarged their communities
only by recruitment campaigns.

that the modern sensibility finds very beautiful. "Good spirits," Lee quite rightly insisted, "will not live where there is dirt." Good spirits left the ugliness of Manchester.

The Shakers were only one of a series of American sects with paradisaical preoccupations, memorably described by Dolores B. Hayden in *Seven American Utopias: The Architecture of Communitarian Socialism, 1790–1975* (1976). Others included the Pennsylvania Moravians (who preferred to be buried vertically since it was space-saving), the Oneida Community (which actually created the "Perfectionist" cult) and the Roycrofters. This last was a commercialized version of the British Arts and Crafts movement, with work ethic pioneer Elbert Hubbard as its colourful huckster-impresario

But the Shakers were the most completely uncompromising in their search for a version of worldly perfection which kept man's ugly appetites for luxury, jewellery, decoration and love in control. "Set not your hearts upon worldly objects," Mother Lee said, "but let this be your labour, to keep a spiritual sense."

Above Photograph by Jack E. Boucher of the Shaker Centre Family Trustees' Office in Mercer County, Kentucky (1963). Harmony was evident in all buildings constructed by the Shakers.

Above A copper dish made by Elbert Hubbard's Roycrofters, East Aurora, New York, c.1900, and a copper and enamelled letterholder, Buffalo Workshops, 1900. A utopian community designed its version of perfection into everyday goods.

Overleaf Interior of the Moravian Church in Bethlehem, Pennsylvania (1948). The Pennsylvania Moravians were one of several American utopian communities who wanted to design a simple life in contrast to the emerging industrial cultures of the big cities. Their capital was Bethlehem, begun when a five hundred acre tract of land was bought near Philadelphia in 1741.

Amazing grace

Mother Lee designed a Heaven on Earth. Her taste for purity was, perhaps, driven as much by an acquired Yankee Puritanism plus post-revolutionary zeal as it was by religious revivalism, communitarianism or any tormented personal agenda based on flight from squalor and sexual abuse. Nonetheless, from 1787 Mother Lee's followers lived as a "family". The design of Shaker furniture and products that began to emerge from New Lebanon was an expression of the family's article of faith that the external form revealed the internal spirit. Once you have the injunction "Let your tables be clean enough to eat on without cloths," the aesthetic necessarily follows.

The most complete expressions of the Shakers' perfectionism were the Meeting Houses, the first being designs of Master Builder Moses Johnson. They were painted white to distinguish them from the work buildings, which were red or yellow. The Shakers created common objects – buckets, baskets, boxes – with amazing grace. Master Cabinet-Maker David Rowley reinvented beauty, or, at least, redefined it as a process of reduction and refinement. The idea was that "A man can show his religion as much in measuring onions as he can in singing glory hallelujah." Charles Dickens visited and was dismayed, but Charles Sheeler, the painter of industrial landscapes, was more enthusiastic. He saw the beautiful democracy of perfectionism: the Shakers "recognised no justifiable difference in the quality of workmanship for any object." Anything could be beautiful, but – as a corollary – nothing may be ugly. Micajah Burnett's Meeting House at Pleasant Hill, completed in 1820, is a response to ugliness, an architectural expression of Heaven on Earth. "Odd or fanciful" styles of architecture must be avoided, the Shakers insisted.

The Shakers had some very strict rules wherein design and morality were inextricable. Bedsteads must be green. Bedspreads may not be checked, striped or in flowery patterns. A looking glass may never be more than 18 inches by 12, otherwise a "Believer" might be tempted into vanity. Curtains may only be white, blue, green or any other "modest" colour.

And there were the Shakers' Rules of Beauty. From these we can, by inference, determine the Shakers' Rules of Ugliness.

1. Regularity is Beautiful.

2. There is great beauty in harmony.

3. Order is the creation of beauty.

4. Beauty rests on utility.

5. All beauty that has not a foundation in use, soon grows distasteful, and needs continuous replacement with something new.

6. That which has the highest use, possesses the greatest beauty.

Opposite Postcard of a Shaker woman fulfilling chair orders at the Shakers' Mount Lebanon furniture shop, NY. (c.1850s), and a Shaker chair with taped seat and a sewing table at the Hancock Shaker village near Pittsfield, Massachusetts. Paradoxically, while the Shakers repudiated industry, the clean lines of their furniture and buildings were keenly admired by twentieth century industrial designers.

The Oneida Community's version of Perfectionism was less austere, more commercial. The founder, a Yale graduate called John Humphrey Noyes (1811–86), was, like Mother Lee, instructed by God to make an Earthly Paradise. In Noyes' interpretation, such a paradise would not only include perfectly designed objects capable of no improvement (the Final Shoe and the Lazy Susan dining table are Oneida achievements), but also "complex marriage". This latter was a licence to liberal and unlimited fornication, vaguely sanctioned by the teachings of the Bible. This practice had them run out of Putney, Vermont.

A memory of ugliness made Ann Lee's Shakers crave the purity of a totally designed environment. It was Heaven on Earth… at least to those with a taste for reductivism. To test the human genius for variety and invention, to calibrate the extremes of beauty as expression of a religious ideal, the purity of a Shaker interior need only be compared to the excess of a Baroque one. Significantly, while the purity of the Shakers was inspired by disgust at the ugliness of dirt and exploitation, the Baroque was also inspired by error. Deformity of one sort or another – psychological or morphological – is central to the Baroque idea.

Thus we see swooning saints with exaggerated gestures and expressions, contorted architectural details and a giddy commitment to emotional and aesthetic extremes. The clarity and control evident in the Shaker aesthetic may have as its source Mother Lee's repugnance for sexuality: this is design as a metaphor of celibacy. But the deformations of Baroque have a sexual character too, although it is orgiastic and orgasmic rather than primly chaste. Baroque is an alternative version of total design: it is deformity made into art. It is excess legitimized. It is another version of Heaven on Earth. And it is quite the opposite of pure. Michael Snodin is a curator at London's Victoria & Albert Museum. He says, "You simply can't have impure Baroque." There is no distorted excess that cannot be accommodated in its aesthetic.

In fact, the Italian word *barocca* means a pearl of irregular shape; an ugly duckling. Significantly, the people who practised what we call Baroque did not possess the word. Its current usage we owe to the Swiss art historian Heinrich Wölfflin, whose book entitled *Renaissance und Barock* was published in 1884. As an expression, it is intended to legitimize that which perhaps, to a Swiss purist eye, was ugly.

A penumbra of bewilderment

Certainly, any aesthetic that depends on discipline and restraint is confounded by the experience of the Baroque. Take, for example, what is perhaps the greatest of all examples of Baroque architecture: the church of Santa Caterina in Palermo. The interior is visually overwhelming or some might say gross. There are queasy *trompe l'œil* ceiling paintings by Filippo Randazzo and Vito d'Anna. Elsewhere, gilt, ceramics, marble, carvings, glass and candles jostle for attention in a crawlingly over-busy assemblage that is either sick-making or breathtaking. Or perhaps it is both.

When he visited, taking notes for the lovely travel book that became *The Golden Honeycomb: a Sicilian Quest* (1951), Vincent Cronin described the Santa Caterina experience as "absolute satisfaction together with a penumbra of bewilderment". There may be an exuberant sexual metaphor struggling to escape from this statement, just as there is a frustrated sexual metaphor contained and restrained in Shaker purity. There may well be no dirt and mess in Heaven, but on Earth there most certainly is. What is certain is that distress and deformation may be components of ugliness, but they are also inspirations of great art. Beauty of madly various types, it seems, can be produced through Leonardo's series of disgusts.

Right Chiesa di Santa Caterina, Palermo. This most remarkable Sicilian Baroque church was begun in 1566. The overwhelming excess and swaggering *trompe l'oeil* of the interior challenge all assumptions about ecclesiastical calm and spiritual comfort. A visit is an aggressive, but thrilling, experience.

2. Ugly Science, or Good Maths, Bad Results

Can ugliness be measured mathematically?
Is science aesthetically neutral?
Are we hard-wired to admire this or that?
Can nastiness ever be beautiful?
If a pig is so useful, why is it ugly?

Science can detect, but cannot define descriptively, what it is that makes something disgusting. Science can tell us the name of a particular ugly quality, but can it describe it? For example, the ugly mixture of bad smell and bad taste that is "corked" wine – defined scientifically, it is 2,4,6 – trichloroanisole, or TCA, a fungoid compound, but this is not the most evocative of descriptions.

There is today an innocent belief that science is morally neutral, but it is nothing of the sort. Literature's most famous illustration of the unease caused by the advance of science was Mary Shelley's *Frankenstein* (1818). Here was a metaphor of science interfering with nature to catastrophic effect. And that effect was horrifyingly ugly. But in truth, Frankenstein's hideous monster was a bit of a poppet. "Everywhere I see bliss, from which I alone am irrevocably excluded," he, if it was in fact a "he", complained.

The emerging discipline of neuroesthetics promises scientific precision where before only culturally conditioned taste and prejudice operated. Neuroesthetics is a term coined by Semir Zeki, author of *Inner Visions* (1999) and a neurosurgeon at University College Hospital, London. The belief of neuroestheticians, especially of Zeki, is that since our perceptions are based on the stimulated activity of neural mechanisms, responses to art can be tested experimentally. If this is so, then our taste is not the product of our acquired education or our inherited proclivities, but the inevitable and true result of electrical energy in the brain, responses to external stimuli. If the neuroesthetic proposition is valid, then ugliness is not a matter of dispute, it is a definable absolute.

A colleague of Zeki's, V. S. Ramachandran argues that there are common factors in all the different types of art favoured in different periods by different cultures. He says, for example: "There might be neurons... that represent sensuous, round feminine form as opposed to angular, masculine form".

Draining enchantment from the world

Some critics, including John Hyman, claim that the neuroesthetic proposition threatens to "drain enchantment from the world". Classical and Renaissance civilizations believed a strictly observed set of proportions would produce beauty in buildings and art. This was an earlier threat of draining enchantment from the world since it suggested that no further

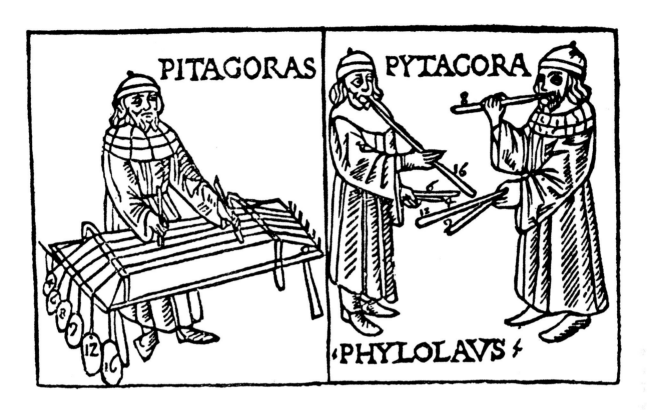

PITAGORAS

PYTAGORA

·PHYLOLAVS·

Above left/right Pythagoras of Samos made the proposition that music has a mathematical explanation. He spoke of the harmony of the spheres and believed that all beautiful experiences are related by rules of proportion. But if beauty has a numerical rationale, can the same be said of ugliness?

experimentation would ever be necessary, as the rules were already established. Similarly, the latest research in brain function suggests there may be a physiological basis for our sense of proportion, our preference for certain shapes and contours. Thanks to the managed transit of observed electrons in laboratory conditions, via sensors clamped to your skull, the mathematical formulae that have preoccupied civilization from Pythagoras to Donald Judd via St Thomas Aquinas may soon be understood to have a basis in the murk of brain chemistry.

Proportions are a rule of mathematical relationships that determine pleasing effects in building and art. Proportions are a way of avoiding ugliness and, as if to demonstrate their profound significance in human affairs, proportional rules seem to apply to music as well as to art and architecture. Pythagoras knew there was a mathematical expression of beautiful sound.

Take, for example, a rectangle whose proportion is 2:1. If you cut pieces of string using this ratio and put them under the same tension, when plucked – as if a stringed instrument – they are exactly an octave apart. Do the same with a rectangle with the proportions of 3:2 and the difference is a fifth. And so it goes on.

The crossover from musical proportion to art appears most obviously in buildings. Architecture is frozen, or at any rate solid music, at least according to Friedrich von Schelling or, in competitive attributions,

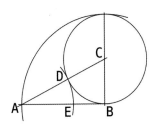

Above The golden section, or the classical *sectio aurea*, is a proportional rule. If a line is divided in a way so that the relationship of the smaller part to the larger is the same as the larger part to the whole, it is a golden section. Mathematically, this is 1.618. Some speculate that we find this ratio pleasing because it corresponds to the human field of vision.

Opposite Andrea Palladio's Villa Malcontenta, Vicenza (1559–61). The architectural equivalent of *bella figura*: perfect poise, good manners, and fine proportions. Palladio's designs are perhaps the most widely admired in the entire history of architecture. No one has ever said: "that's an ugly Palladio!"

Overleaf This sunflower's heart shows how many natural forms evolve in a way that can be described by maths. The number of petals and the angle at which seeds grow often relates to the Fibonacci Sequence. Fibonacci was the name acquired by Leonardo of Pisa whose *Liber Abaci* (1202) defined a pattern of growth first noticed by Sanskrit scholars. The Fibonacci Sequence has each new number as the sum of its precedents. The properties created by this sequence are generally pleasing.

to Goethe. More certain is that Palladio's proportions would have been recognized by Pythagorean musicians: the Villa Malcontenta, Palladio's masterpiece, could have been measured and transcribed as a melody. But the curious thing is, the resulting sound may have been ugly. Palladio worked on Pythagorean principles: start with a square floor plan. Draw a diagonal and drop it to make a new longer room in the proportions of 1: square root of 2. This is visually pleasing, but musical notes in the same proportion produce an interval called an augmented fourth which most people find disagreeable. This sort of dissonance – this sort of ugly sound – was known as *diabolus in musica*, or the devil in music. So here again is an association of ugliness with evil.

But the laws of proportion don't seem to work across both music and architecture. One to the square root of two is exactly the same proportion as a sheet of (perfectly proportioned?) A4 paper. This paper-sizing modulus – first proposed by the physician Georg Christoph Lichtenberg in 1786 – has the nearly magical quality that when you halve it, by folding or cutting, the proportions remain intact. This beautiful logic appealed strongly to the mentality of the French Revolutionaries and the modern acceptance of these proportions dates from 1798, although it was only codified in 1922. This was when DIN, or Deutsche Industrie Normen, the German Industrial Standard, laid down the particulars of paper size and proportion. DIN 476 made Pythagorean proportions (and the A4 size of 210 x 297) the norm for Europeans.

So it is a wonderful thing when the mystical music of the spheres meets earth-bound stationery to create practical beauty. If concepts of harmony are important to beauty then, by extension, concepts of dissonance must be fundamental to an idea of ugliness. The most familiar proportional formula in art and architecture is the Golden Section, the *section aurea* of the Romans. This is an irrational mathematical constant, closely related in shape and rhythm to the Fibonacci series. (The latter is a sequence of numbers in which, starting with zero and one and going on to two, the resulting composites are the sum of the two preceding numbers.)

It is informally expressed as a line divided up in such a way that, at least according to Euclid, the area contained by the smaller section and whole equals that of the square of the larger section. Or, to put it another way: the proportion of 8:13. Or yet another way, 1.6180339887, often called a beautiful or even a divine number. Its place in modern history we owe to Luca Pacioli's *De divina proportione* (1509). Mathematicians talk of the generating polynomial of the recursion, but a real-world interpretation of the Golden Section and why we find it satisfying suggests that the proportions 8:13 are almost exactly the same as the proportions of the field of vision of the human eye. Satisfy these proportions and we find things pleasing; ignore them and the result is ugliness.

There is an uneasy relationship between architecture and science, even if, more so than the other arts, architecture, to be practically successful, must respond to physical laws that can be described in strict mathematical terms. Occasionally this finds expression, first in poetry and criticism. Coventry Patmore, the Victorian critic, to suggest an odd example, believed that beauty in architecture is the expression of gravitational thrust: thus the enigma of beauty in buildings is explained by a straightforward physical principle. By extension, ugliness in architecture might be explained by a building's design ignoring the inevitable vectors of gravity. This may be why we find the swooping curves of featurism or other meretricious architectural effects unsettling. More recently, Le Corbusier, reviled by people who have not read his work as a calculating mechanist determined to leach humanity from building design so we can all live the emotional lives of concrete pumps, developed a system of proportions based on the human body. This he called *Modulor* and published in book form in 1948. It is based on human proportions, which are themselves closely related to the Fibonacci sequence. The architect writes of his invention: "Rhythms apparent to the eye and clear in their relations with one another. And these rhythms are at the very root of human activities. They resound in man by an organic inevitability".

Science does not recognise the idea of beauty or ugliness, although mathematicians often describe an equation as "beautiful" if it is elegant and correct. "A mathematician's pattern must be beautiful," G. H. Hardy wrote in 1904. "Beauty is the first test: there is no permanent place in the world for ugly mathematics". An ugly equation would be, in this reckoning, clumsy and wrong. Researchers also sometimes describe results of experiments as "beautiful". While the science itself may aspire to neutrality, the choice of words perhaps reveals something fundamental in the architecture of the human brain: even a dry calculus can be beautiful if it is intellectually pleasing. This rather suggests that the source of beauty might lie in concepts rather than appearances. Thus, the absolute perfection of Pythagoras's Theorem. Could anyone find one over root two ugly?

So too with ugliness itself. Does it reside in the concept rather than the carapace? Successful machines are assumed to follow the laws of science. But can a machine which follows these laws with grim efficiency ever claim to be "beautiful", irrespective of its purpose? Can a weapon be beautiful? Guns are often cited as examples of perfect function, as if the efficient discharge of a lethal bullet somehow inevitably reveals perfect form. In the matter of dealing with death, frivolity has no place. Rather as architecture must describe gravity, so a gun must describe ballistics.

Opposite Le Corbusier's Modulor, as shown in *Science et Vie* (October, 1955). So far from being the inhumane mechanist his critics deride, Le Corbusier was fascinated by anthropometric proportion in the tradition of Leonardo. His book *Le Modulor* (1948) was inspired by a commission from the Association Francaise de Normalisation, the French government standards agency.

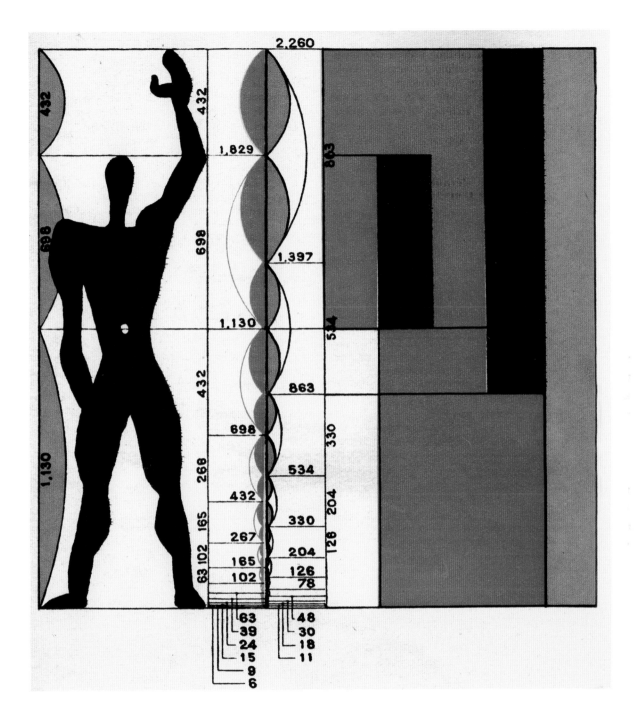

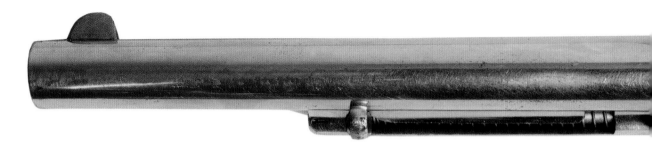

Happiness is a well-designed gun

The Colt .45 has a place in many histories of design: its ingenious modular construction allowed it to be manufactured inexpensively and in large numbers. It became a symbol of the pioneer spirit on the American frontier: severely undecorated, an expression of unblinking purposiveness, it stood out with dignity from the mass of cynically artificed mid-nineteenth-century production. Yet the Colt's purpose was to mutilate and kill and to subjugate the spirit. It is, of course, by accident or design, very well proportioned.

Less ambiguous in its ugly, destructive intention, to offer an example of great technical efficiency producing something very ugly, was the "broom-handle Mauser" M1912 machine-gun with its gross and distended form, made more unsettling by the fine gentility of its detail. Or the infamous Vickers Mark I heavy machine-gun whose purpose was to turn German infantry into red mist on an industrial basis. Produced from 1912 to 1945, the Vickers set a world record for non-stop firing at 450 rounds per minute. Look at the pawl depressor on the right-hand side under the feedway. The work of the devil? Or the horrible Victorian elaboration of the cloth jacket, like puttees covering an ugly snout.

Above Samuel Colt's Patent Firearms Manufacturing Company was established at Hartford, Connecticut, in 1836. The radical simplicity and refined elegance of his designs impressed visitors to The Great Exhibition of 1851. The "Peacemaker" was, of course, designed for aggression. A thing of great beauty, with an ugly purpose.

Left A Vickers machine gun on a tripod, c.1912. A development of the Maxim gun, the Vickers achieved astonishing levels of reliability. During one action in 1916 the Machine Gun Corps fired a million rounds in 12 hours without intermission or breakdown. This was, perhaps, the ultimate perversion of the industrial process.

Above and overleaf A B-52
taxiing at Edwards Air Force Base
(CA) and in its graveyard. The
Boeing B-52 Stratofortress went
into service in 1955 and became
known as the "Big Ugly Fat
Fucker". The Strategic Arms
Limitation Talks required the
USAF to stand-down most of its
B-52 fleet. They were parked in the
Arizona desert so that Soviet
satellites could test compliance.
The image is haunting and elegiac.

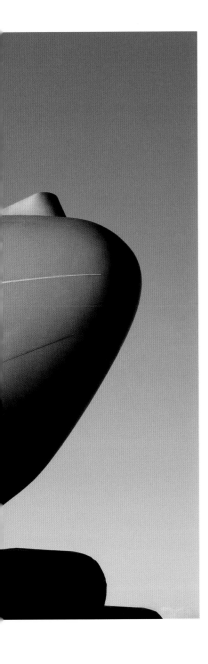

The B-52: an appreciation

Can an aircraft, combining architecture's respect for gravity with a gun's merciless functionalism, ever be beautiful? Certainly, Le Corbusier thought so. As a reprimand to his contemporary architects who found themselves slaves to decoration, he said *L'avion accuse!* Which is to say, the aircraft points the finger of blame and, at the same time, points the way to a future of beautiful architecture. Provided only, that is, that architects respect the same laws of nature which keep several tons of aluminium precariously airborne.

The Boeing B-52, originally known as the Stratofortress, was the perfect expression of America's post-war vision, which magnificently, or disgustingly (it is a matter of taste) combined geopolitical imperialism, science fiction, flashy styling and the cowboy mentality. The programme was the dream of Air Force General Curtis LeMay, and it was realized in the post-VE Day euphoria. The prototype flew on 15 April 1952 and the pilot was a good old boy called "Tex" Johnson.

As aeronautical science, the B-52 is supreme. In moral terms, it is repugnant. Whether it is ugly we will decide a little further down the page. Conceived as the ultimate Cold War deterrent, the B-52 was designed to carry 32,000kg of conventional high-explosive ordnance (although the later G and H models carried 20 AGM-69 SRAM nukes). In 1965, the B-52 fleet was modified so it could go carpet-bombing and various horrible records of atrocity were later set in Vietnam. During Operation Linebacker II, to name just one unpleasant example, there was the 1972 Christmas bombing of Hanoi and Haiphong where over 12 days and 729 sorties, B-52s dropped 15,237 tons of bombs. Until terrifyingly recently, B-52s carrying sublime volumes of destructive, murderous, nuclear matter were continuously circling the globe, loitering with airborne menace to deposit horror on whomsoever. But while the purpose is nasty, the technical achievements are pleasing. In the first Gulf War, B-52s flew the longest mission ever: a 14,000-mile roundtrip. In a late gesture of environmental awareness, B-52s were the first USAF aircraft to fly with Syntroleum's Fischer-Tropsch synthetic fuel, a small nod to environmental awareness by a machine that has the capability to destroy the entire planet.

Among the adepts of the USAF, the B-52 was known as BUFF, an affectionate acronym for Big Ugly Fat Fucker. Certainly, the size of the craft is as frightening as its purpose. It has something of the sublime about it. In Burke's *Philosophical Enquiry into the Origins of our Ideas of the Sublime and the Beautiful* (1757), the definition of the sublime includes terror, obscurity, power, privation, vastness, infinity, magnitude, loudness and suddenness. Oh, yes, and the "cries of animals".

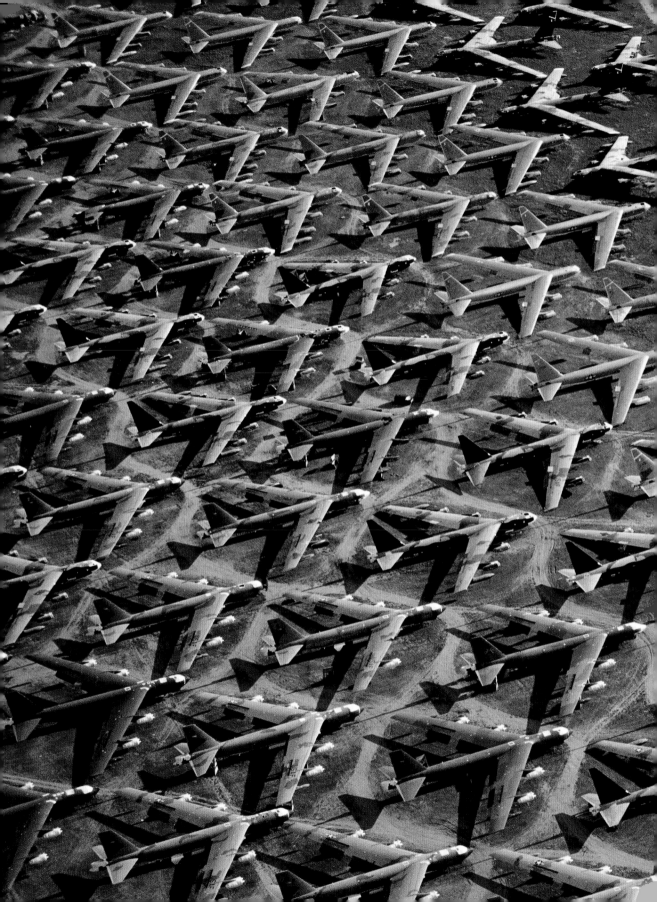

The bulk of the sublime B-52 fleet, redundant after the end of the Cold War, now sits retired in the dry heat of the Arizona desert at Davis-Monthan Air Force Base near Tucson. Seen from the air these abandoned aircraft present a compelling spectacle; here is a military industrial graveyard. Lined up in echelon, the patterns of the grounded B-52s have the elegiac aspect of fallen warriors. Who could say whether this sight is a beautiful or an ugly one?

Admirably calculated

If functionality were a test of beauty, then the B-52 would qualify. But in his famous book Burke has a wonderful passage about the functionality of the pig and how the farmyard animal fails the test for beauty: "For on that principle, the wedge-like snout of a swine, with its tough cartilage at the end, the little sunk eyes, and the whole make of the head, so well adapted to its offices of digging and rooting would be extremely beautiful". Similar arguments apply to monkeys: "Admirably calculated for running, leaping, grappling and climbing; and yet there are few animals which seem to have less beauty". In nature and in science there is no clear relationship between functionalism and beauty… nor between efficiency and ugliness.

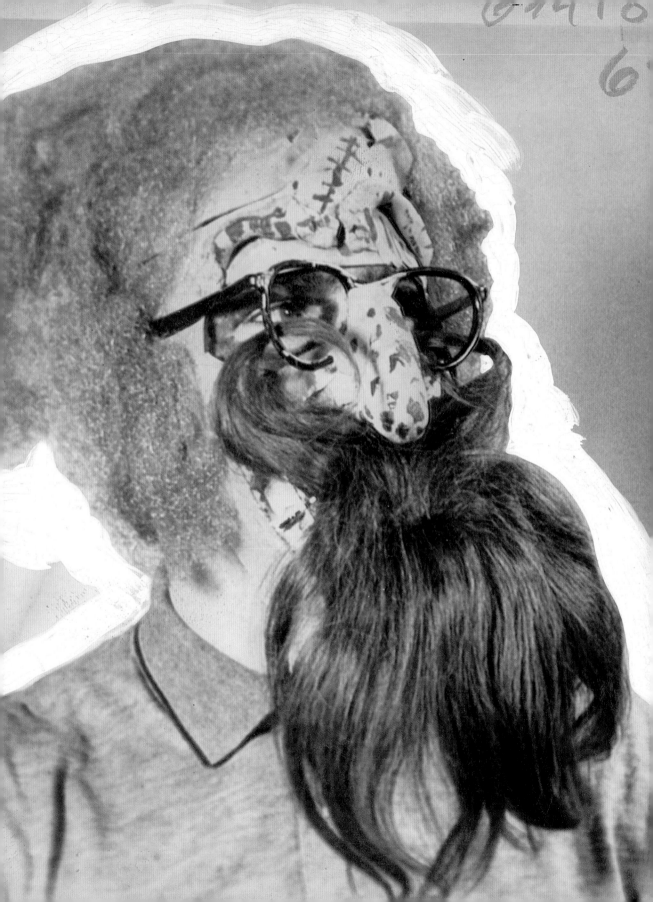

3. Manners, or The Ugly Customer

Opposite A contestant in the University of Maryland's "Ugliest Man on Campus" Contest, 1969. Vanity moves us in strange, competitive ways.

Is ugliness more than skin-deep?
How to explain why ugliness is not unpopular?
Is beauty boring?

Are people ugly? Well, their language certainly can be. To the Anglophone eye and ear, Italian sounds beautiful, but the Polish language seems discordant. A recent study in art history (by Piotr Bernatowicz, Kracow, 2006), plucked at random from a reference book, seems to bear this out. It was titled *Picasso za żelazną kurtyną. Recepcja artysty i jego sztuki w krajach Europy Środkowo-Wschodniej w latach.*

Some cultures seem to have a positive will to ugliness. Even by the shocking standards of Stalinist architecture elsewhere in Eastern Europe, Polish buildings of the mid twentieth century seem notably bleak or distressingly swaggering. If beauty is a golden mean, halfway between middle and extreme, as Robert Herrick suggested, then in recent years Poles have rarely achieved it. And the implication is that ugliness is at the extremes.

An old Polish joke says there is no such thing as an ugly woman, only a lack of vodka. This may be evidence of an awareness that ugliness is a matter of national identity. Besides Poland, there is Portugal. Even given the wilful deformations that characterize the style in Italy and Spain, Portuguese Baroque architecture seems especially demanding. The deformations are extreme without being exciting; it is almost as if there is a national will to disturb. Similarly, while the sound of Spanish is euphonious to Anglo ears, the sound of neighbouring Portuguese – which is much more nasal, guttural and harsh – seems ugly.

Style – the dress of thought

Language provides special insights into the rules of ugliness.

In his magisterial *The King's English* (1906), Fowler explains what's meant by brachylogy, a figure of speech that's a useful abbreviation, thus avoiding an "ugly string of words". So here is a repetition of the idea that beauty is in some way related to economy. Fowler, in his *Dictionary of English Usage* (1926) also mentions the rare term "uglily", saying only that this word, ugly in itself, is "less rare than most adverbs ending in -lily". Quite so.

In language, ugliness is the opposite of style. "Proper words in proper places make the true definition of style," says Swift in an early defence of the functionalist idea. So an ugly sentence is one full of irrelevant allusions and vulgarizing adaptations. Style, an old saying goes, is the feather that makes the arrow fly straight, not the feather you put in your cap.

So, following the flight of this thought, ugliness may be what makes you speak clumsily, or aggressively because in the Southern United States "don't be ugly with me" means "stop being rude". In the Northern United States, "ugly" is sometimes applied to cattle or horses that are hard to manage. Ugly moods, rumours, tempers and clouds extend the meaning to threatening and ominous.

But what of physical ugliness and its suggestions of repulsion? The idea that beauty is boring is a recurrent one, and this may be based in the idea that economy and moderation are essential to it. Beauty cannot be an extreme. Scott Fitzgerald's remark that "after a certain degree of prettiness one pretty girl is as pretty as another" is revealing of a curious human truth: while we deplore ugliness, we crave its remedial effect. Ugly is interesting.

The Ugly Duchess (only skin-deep)

For most, but not all, of civilization, art has been concerned with capturing and defining the beautiful, however construed. Yet perversely, we have no artist's image of the most famous beauty of them all: Helen of Troy. Her abduction by Paris gave rise to the Trojan Wars and, perhaps significantly, "abduction" is a euphemism. Abduction sounds rather fine and elegant; the act to which Helen was subject was in fact *raptus*, the more ugly rape.

The Greek painter Zeuxis (active fifth century BC) struggled with the problems of portraying overwhelming beauty, but, alas, we have no record of his efforts. Images of Helen and her abductor/rapist in action occur often on Attic red-figure vases, but nowhere do we see a face that is anything more than a caricature. Still, the idea of Helen's sensational beauty – a beauty that could start wars – is a commonplace in European civilization.

The face that launched a thousand quotations

And this unknown figure of Helen inspired one of the great poetic lines about beauty. In Christopher Marlowe's *The Tragicall History of Doctor Faustus* (1592), the wretched hero is indulging in the fruits of his compact with the Devil. In exchange for the long-term future of his soul, Faust has entered into an unwise short-term arrangement where, over 24 years, he has access to all the world's knowledge and pleasures. One of the latter is the sight of the most beautiful woman who ever lived. So the Devil's agent, Mephistopheles, arranges for Helen to appear. "Is this the face that launched a thousand ships?" Faust asks, referring to the naval exercise of the Trojan Wars. Maybe Faust was disappointed with ultimate beauty.

Right Helen of Troy: a face so beautiful she launched a thousand ships, according to Christopher Marlowe. One of the first images of Helen (c.540BC) from a black-figure amphora. Biochemistry professor Isaac Asimov advocated the creation of the *millihelen*, defined as a measure of beauty sufficient to launch a single ship.

Overleaf left Bust of *Helen of Troy* by French sculptor Jean Baptiste Clesinger (1868).

Overleaf right Quentin Massys' *A Grotesque Old Woman* (or The Ugly Duchess) (c.1513), oil on oak. Massys' astonishing picture may be related to Leonardo's studies of grotesque heads. The sitter is now diagnosed as suffering from Paget's Disease, a deformation of the bones. With magnificent absurdity, The Ugly Duchess is one of the most popular postcards sold in London's National Gallery shop.

Using Marlowe's line as inspiration, Isaac Asimov coined the term *millihelen*, which is the unit of beauty necessary to launch a single ship.

The astonishing popularity of Quentin Massys' 1513 portrait of Margaret of Austria, entitled *An Old Woman*, in London's National Gallery – it is a best-selling postcard in the shop – demonstrates the curious law that ugliness is by no means necessarily repugnant. On the contrary, this grotesquely malformed woman, conventionally known as *The Ugly Duchess* and the inspiration for Tenniel's scary illustrations in *Alice in Wonderland*, is among the most popular pictures with visitors to Trafalgar Square.

Disease had a cruel fascination for painters of the northern Renaissance. Massys' sitter is suffering from *osteitis deformans*, known as Paget's Disease. This is a metabolic abnormality that deforms the bones. Normally, it affects the lower body, but here the sitter presents symptoms in her face. In this case the enlarged upper jaw has led to a hideously distended lip and a scrunched-up nose. Her forehead and chin are also distended and, one might assume, so too are the collarbone and arms.

The portrait was once assumed to be a fantastic grotesque, an imaginary composition inspired perhaps by Massys' acquaintance Leonardo da Vinci – but is now thought to be a faithful observation from nature, no matter how unfortunate. X-ray analysis has shown that Massys made meticulous changes during the progress of the painting. We know that Massys and Leonardo were acquainted and exchanged drawings, but this process of continuous improvement might not have occurred if he were only adapting a Leonardo original.

Warts and all

Disease was also an influence on another famous portrait. A wart is a small, rough, disfiguring tumour caused by the human papillomavirus (HPV). The Lord Protector of England, Oliver Cromwell, suffered from them. And since an important element of Cromwell's projection of self was Puritan honesty, as opposed to the Cavalier vanity he made it his business to remove from the catalogue of optional behaviour, warts were not to be ignored. Disfiguringly ugly as they might be.

Be that as it may, the painter Sir Peter Lely (who on the Restoration became Charles II's Principal Painter in Ordinary) had a professional inclination to flattery. So when commissioned to make a portrait of Cromwell, he chose to disguise the presenting symptoms of HPV. This, a century later, gave rise to what became a famous exchange. A conversation between the Duke of Buckingham and his architect, William Winde, was overheard by the gossipy Horace Walpole and recorded in his *Anecdotes of Painting in England* (1764). Here, we learn that Cromwell said, "Mr. Lely,

Opposite Lewis Carroll's *Alice's Adventures in Wonderland* (1865) featured a Duchess inspired by Quentin Massys' painting, the stuff of many childhood nightmares. Carroll coined the term "uglification".

Overleaf left Human papillomavirus cells, the cause of disfiguring warts.

Overleaf right Sir Peter Lely, *Oliver Cromwell* (c.1660), oil on canvas. The Lord Protector allegedly refused to be flattered in his portrait and commissioned Lely to paint "all these roughnesses, pimples, warts and everything you see," hence the phrase "warts and all". It is assumed that this version is a posthumous portrait.

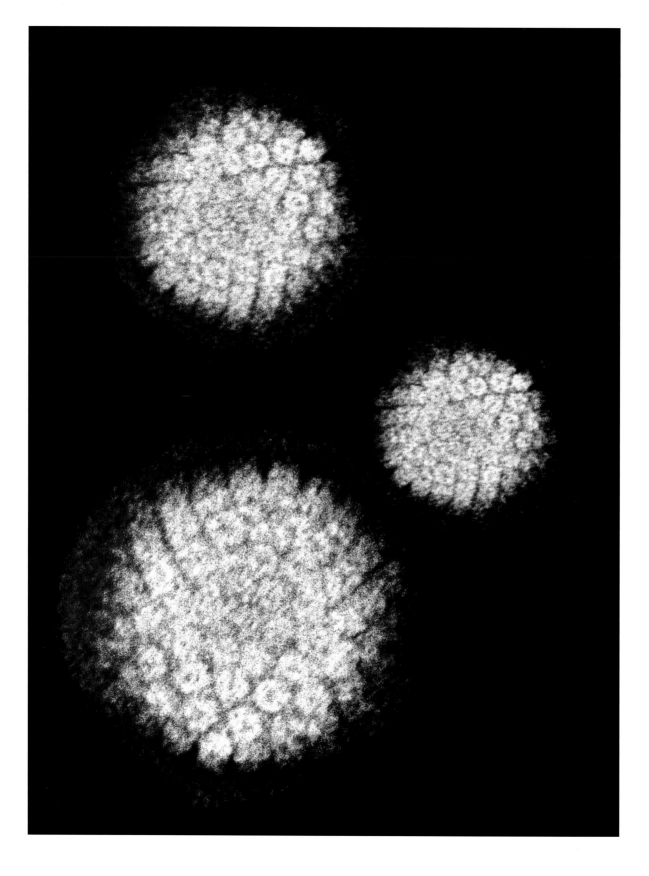

1259 PARIS. - Notre-Dame. - Chimère. - Chimaera. - ND

I desire you would use all your skill to paint your picture truly like me, and not flatter me at all; but remark all these roughness, pimples, warts and everything as you see me. Otherwise, I will never pay you a farthing for it". Sixty years later, one Alpheus Cary of Massachusetts redacted this as Cromwell insisting he be portrayed "warts and all". Thus the wart became a sort of eponym for a voluntary declaration of the ugly. Beauty may be truth, but so too is ugliness.

Gargoyles: towards a new theory

We find grotesques more fascinating than disturbing. The affection felt for gargoyles is, surely, evidence of how pleasing ugliness can be. A gargoyle is a humanoid grotesque incorporated into medieval architecture, often, but not always, as a disguise for a rainwater spout. The most famous examples are in the Galerie des Chimères in Notre-Dame; modern gargoyles also appear on Manhattan's Chrysler Building, although they are decorative rather than functional. We get the word from the French term *gargouille,* meaning throat, although Gargouille was also the name of the terrifying

Above left to right The ugly in everyday life. Gargoyles from Notre-Dame de Paris. Lions, dogs, snakes, eagles and occasional composite chimaeras, gargoyles are grotesque carved figures. Medieval in association, they were known in ancient Greece and in Jazz Age Manhattan. Their threatening aspect was designed to repel evil spirits, although St Bernard of Clairvaux called them idolatrous "unclean monkeys". Gargoyles disappeared from English architecture when the London Building Act of 1724 made downpipes mandatory and gargoyle waterspouts redundant.

PARIS. — Notre-Dame. — Chimère.

57-E. B.

ND Phot

Above right A photograph by Oscar Graubner of American photographer and journalist Margaret Bourke-White perching on an eagle head gargoyle at the top of the Chrysler Building and focussing a camera, New York (1935).

Overleaf Lord Voldemort, the evil wizard who is Harry Potter's enemy. He has a skeletal appearance, red eyes, snake nostrils, bad teeth and a pale, bald head.

dragon that lived in the river Seine near Rouen.

And because of their specific purpose in architecture, gargoyles did indeed gargle. Given that their function was to act as decorative features diverting rainwater from ecclesiastical roofs, here is a curious example of wilful ugliness and useful function deliberately combined. The 1725 London Building Act made downpipes obligatory, effectively ending the life of the gargoyle in Britain. It is curious that just as the word "ugly" was making its tentative entry into the English language – just as the Industrial Revolution was about to make ugliness a matter of debate – so the most familiar expressions of the grotesque were legislated out of existence.

A taste for the horrible

Gargoyles were endearing, but the mentality of the Middle Ages was perhaps better able to deal with ugliness on a daily basis. To the industrial or post-industrial mind, ugliness is readily associated with evil and fear. In his *Choix de maxims consolantes sur l'amour* (1846), Baudelaire explained "pleasure in the face of ugliness comes from a mysterious feeling which is the thirst for

the unknown and the taste for the horrible". Hence Lord Voldemort in the *Harry Potter* movies has bad teeth, nasty little slits where his nostrils should be, a menacing bald head and an alabaster complexion.

Now, as the word "beauty" has been banned from some American campuses on account of its implied elitism, so ugliness is going through a partial rehabilitation. Or if rehabilitation is not the right word, ideas about ugliness are at least being consciously reviewed. Some argue that our disturbance over who is and who is not an ugly customer is one of the last discriminatory prejudices. Indeed, San Francisco and Washington have civic ordinances forbidding professional discrimination on aesthetic grounds.

A paper entitled "Beauty and the Labor Market" was published in the *American Economic Review* in 1994. It argued that the so-called "beauty premium" meant that ugly people earned up to 10 per cent less than those better favoured by nature. Although, frustratingly, it did not define beauty or ugliness in a way that Human Resources might use to help avoid discrimination. A Canadian sociologist called Anthony Synott says: "It hasn't been politically correct to talk about uglyism. But there's no reason for us to think that beautiful people are actually good and ugly people evil, yet we do".

Short people got no reason to live

There may be a Darwinian explanation of our, sometimes, negative responses to ugly customers. And since a Darwinian explanation often includes an element of sex, it goes rather like this. Attractive children display premium genetic material. If attractive children grow up into attractive adults, they may find it easier to develop agreeable interpersonal communications skills because their audience reacts more favourably to them.

So if one version of beauty is only a matter of dermatological superficiality, the effects of personal beauty have profound social (and indeed professional) consequences that are more than skin deep. There is a fine Randy Newman lyric that says: "Short people got no reason to live". In this beauty-related employment theory, short people are also less likely to get a good job. Darwin's argument that evolutionary forces favour a certain physical type may be proven in the job market.

Sexual selection may advance the physical type we call beautiful and if this is true, then the continued existence of the ugly customer is a defiant and disturbing threat to human progress.

Surely ugliness denies the compelling logic of evolution with its nuanced argument that we are ever tending towards to perfection? And how revealing is it of our disturbances that the Surrealists, who claimed access to the sources of motivation, often found the sexual act disgusting? Salvador Dalí told his biographer Fleur Cowles that "eroticism must always be ugly".
(Dalí may not have known that the difference between pornography and

Above Press photograph of the
first lady, Mamie Eisenhower with
Mrs. Fleur Cowles promoting a
fundraising event at the Waldorf
Astoria (1952). The much-married
journalist-socialite Cowles,
biographer of Salvador Dali,
was told by the surrealist that
"eroticism must always be ugly".

eroticism is the lighting.) And Georges Bataille wrote in 1957: "No-one doubts the ugliness of the sexual act… the ugliness of coupling plunges us into anxiety". Well, some more than others.

Plain Jane, jolie-laide and plug ugly

But absolutes of ugliness and beauty are impossible to determine, although the French – with all the philosophical sophistication for which they are famous – have attempted a splendid conceptual compromise. This is the *jolie-laide*, a woman who is at once pretty, but also ugly. Here in this simple but compelling paradox is the delicate balance of our sensibilities. Rather as eroticism is distinguished from pornography only by the subtlety of the lighting, so ugliness can be appealing. The English tend to describe an ugly woman as "plain", a choice of words betraying both a Puritan inheritance and a nice reluctance to cause offence. But it is a concept of much less subtlety than the French *jolie-laide*. For the plain English woman there is little scope

Above London's Ugly Modelling Agency was founded in 1969 by a group of advertising executives and a "pert blonde" who found beauty boring, and instead had models on their books who had "faces with character"– and broken noses, twisted faces and cauliflower ears. It remains in business today.

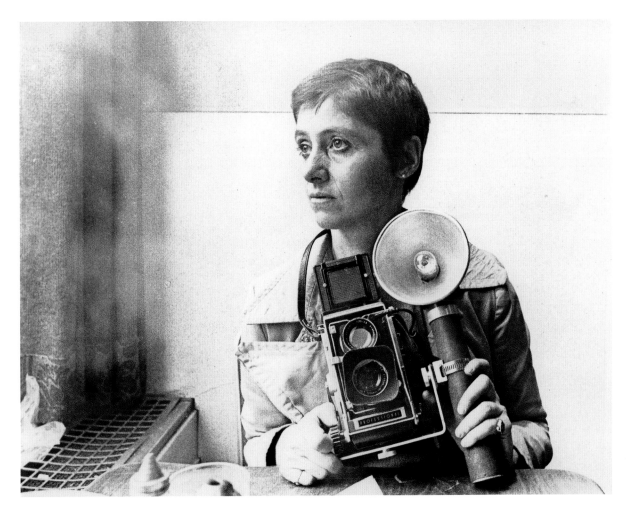

Above Photographer Diane Arbus posing for a rare portrait in the Automat at Sixth Avenue, between 41st & 42nd Street, New York (photograph by Roz Kelly, c.1968). Could Arbus's insistent exposure to a world of freaks and unfortunates have contributed to her suicidal tendencies?

for aesthetic redemption; the French *jolie-laide* exists, by contrast, in a world with a range of value, where attraction and repulsion are on a grey scale.

The black and white photography of Diane Arbus and Richard Avedon presents a compelling greyscale of human potential for misery and joy, ugliness and beauty and any other beatitude of appearance and mood you would care to nominate. Both were born in New York in 1923. Avedon died there in 2004 after a life taking elegant photographs of the beautiful people. Arbus rather preferred the damned, the ugly customers. She committed suicide in 1971 (with drugs and a razor).

Did Arbus's continuous exposure to an underworld of freakery which she recorded with a faithful gloom contribute to her depressed and suicidal state? If voluntary, her taste for deformity and unsettling weirdness was also nonetheless obsessive. Did Avedon's life with Vogue models and rock stars secure for him a more pleasing existence? Is there really a difference between Avedon's elegant portraits of Mick and Bob and Arbus's awful *Jewish Giant at Home with his Parents in the Bronx* (1970)?

If there is, it is not one that either science or art can detect.

4. Heaven and Hell, or Cleanliness, Godliness and their Opposites

What does the landscape of anxiety look like?
Must industry be ugly?
A natural dystopia or an artificial paradise?

Is Heaven beautiful? And is Hell and the Devil's domain ugly?

The conceptual link between cleanliness and godliness, between beauty and goodness and between ugliness and evil is pre-Christian. Perhaps it is even older. In the third century BC, the neo-Platonist Plotinus was considering ugly souls (rather as William Burroughs had been concerned about Sioux ugly spirits). The Greeks had important concepts of monstrosity and error, factors that could produce ugliness. For them, beauty had a moral character. A good soul would inhabit a beautiful body. And, indeed, the opposite held true as well.

Ideas that link divine beneficence with beauty are fundamental to western culture. When during Day Six of Genesis God saw that all He had made was good, He took a rest. "He has made everything beautiful," it says in Ecclesiastes 3:11. Badness was, at this stage, not in His plan. And naturally, before the Fall wickedness and ugliness did not exist on Earth. So when it was invented, Hell needed to be distinctively different to the soothing landscapes of Eden or Paradise.

Opposite The serial killer Myra Hindley, who with partner Ian Brady committed the notorious "Moors murders," at her trial in 1966. Does wickedness express itself externally? For many years this was the belief of criminal psychologists.

As ugly as sin

Just as the mind readily makes a connection between concepts of wickedness and ugliness, so justice and beauty have a symmetrical relationship in our imagination. Truth and beauty also were linked even before Keats made their famous equation: medieval theologians maintained that an image of Satan might be beautiful, provided only that it was a faithful reproduction of his ugliness.

The design of Hell is eloquently revealing of human anxiety. Predella panels on Renaissance altarpieces, especially in the chilly Protestant north of Europe where Hell was a greater preoccupation of painters than in the sunny Catholic south, often show souls struggling with the melodramatic horrors of eternal damnation. But apart from the occasional style pointer, such as Hell being a place where the "worm dieth not", the Bible has very few detailed descriptions of Hell. Perhaps this is because before the 18th and 19th centuries nothing really Hellish had been seen on earth.

Such Biblical descriptions of Hell as there are tend to concentrate on abstractions, although fire is a recurrent motif. So we get outer darkness, brimstone (the common vernacular name for sulphur, as found in the

Right *The Witch no. 1* lithograph by Joseph Baker (1892). The Salem Witch Trials took place between 1692 and 1693. The inquisition was a classic of mass hysteria: the community believed all misfortunes were the work of Satan. This had a crude equivalence with the notion that beauty is goodness. Traditionally, witches are presented in art as ugly and aggressive creatures.

King James version of Genesis), burning winds, fiery ovens, eternal punishment and pits of torment. Here you might find the damned who would be occupied in smoke, weeping and gnashing of teeth and a general clamour of unpleasantness that denied them any possibility of rest. And the reasons for being sent to Hell in the first place are a catalogue of human error and vice which might well serve as a catalogue of ugly behaviour. The list includes idolatry, theft, swindling, discord, dissensions, lying, sorcery, slander, abomination, adultery, greed, impurity, jealousy, factiousness and envy, cowardice, sexual immodesty, hatred, murder, prostitution, drunkenness, witchcraft, fits of rage, orgies, unbelief, homosexuality and ambition.

Almost all accumulated wisdom, fear and prejudice concerning the specification and style of Hell was summarized by Dante in his *Inferno*. Saverio Bettinelli's *Lettere virgiliane* (1758) complained about the ugliness of Dante with all those terrible circles and pits, of bubbling lava and eternal fire. In Dante's ninth or innermost circle of Hell, there is a frozen lake of blood and guilt. When Gustave Doré illustrated Dante in 1867 he brought to the original's late medieval summary of the horrors of Hell an additional iconography derived from his own experience of the urban and industrial horrors of nineteenth-century Paris and London.

A load of old Bosch

Two northern painters of the sixteenth century made a disproportionate contribution to the specifics of our vision of Hell and the ugliness it accommodated. They share a fascination with deformity and disease. Nowhere are visions of Hell painted with more bravura invention and fearless exploitation of available sources than in the fantastical pictures of Hieronymus Bosch and Matthias Grünewald (in fact, Gotthardt: the Grünewald, or "Green Wood", name was a pleasant fiction of 1675).

Bosch painted *The Garden of Earthly Delights,* now in the Prado, Madrid, in the very first years of the sixteenth century. He was a member of the conservative Confraternity of Our Lady and while scholars debate the precise meanings of his fantastical compositions, it's reasonable to assume that his hallucinatory pictures were created as reforming manifestos. They were directed against the depravities of lust. In Bosch's diseased day, sex was ugly.

The right-hand panel of the triptych shows Hell. It seems whole cities are on fire or smouldering. People are being tormented and tortured. Some of them are defecating and vomiting in a most unappealing fashion. When we see a musical score on someone's buttocks or see someone crucified on a harp, it is to indicate that lust is "the music of the flesh". There are mutations, body parts and grotesques. The famous Tree Man is made of a broken egg, and a monster with a bird's head is, we assume, The Prince of Hell. *The Garden of Earthly Delights* can be read on very many levels, but its meaning is unambiguous: Hell is realistic. It contains all the ugly, frightening and deformed things we see on Earth.

Some say it is herpes, but the inspiration for Grünewald's Isenheim Altarpiece was ergotism, a fungal infection that contaminates wheat and rye and, in humans, leads to hallucinations, gastroenteritis and dry gangrene. It was common, which is not to say popular, in the Middle Ages. Sufferers felt as if they were being burned alive and, just to make it worse, fingers, toes and hands might drop off. The unsurprising result was that ergotism produced a sort of delirious madness, not altogether unpleasant.

The Isenheim Altarpiece was commissioned from Grünewald by Antonite monks in 1512 and completed in 1516. St Anthony (251–357), patron saint of Gubbio, was the founder of Christian monasticism and chose mostly to live in a cave (near modern Dayr al-Maymun) where he confronted his many and restless demons. He used austerity to battle his spiritual foes. This principled stand was an inspiration to the many painters who fashioned ever more horrible torments for Anthony, a subject also treated by Bosch. Thus, ergotism was known as St Anthony's Fire. As a result, St Anthony was often invoked by sufferers from skin disease, who gained access to the saint through solemnizing flowerpots of *l'erba di San Antonio* by placing them in sunlight.

Opposite Hieronymous Bosch, *Triptych of the Garden of Earthly Delights* , oil on wood (c.1490–1510). The right-hand panel of the triptych shows Hell. Nothing is known of Bosch's sources or intentions, but it may be assumed that this depiction of horrible disfigurements and mutations is an allegory of temptation and its punitive results: it is night, beauty is banished, the waters are frozen, and there are explosions.

Above left/right Mathias Grünewald, the Isenheim Altarpiece (1516), oil on panel. Grünewald's *magnum opus* is a masterclass in skin disease. Before the interventions of modern medicine, sufferers from ergotism had no possibility of cure this side of the grave. Their disfiguring torments were made into a visual sermon about beauty and ugliness.

The industrial Hell of John Ruskin, or that fatal newness

Doré's illustrations of Dante's *Inferno* were, inadvertently, an illustration of the psychology of the most remarkable art and social critic of the nineteenth century: John Ruskin. A constipated piety and an even more constipated sexual identity put Ruskin continuously in mind of extremes. In his orotund, Biblical cadences he was the Victorian age's most articulate advocate of beauty, and also its most pitiless critic of the new ugliness that industrialization had brought. Hell was never far from his mind.

How curious that in Britain persuasive rural myths were incompatible with the idea of industrialized "progress", while in the America of Henry Ford they were not. Indeed, Ford saw no inconsistency in promoting the decent values of puritan America while also perfecting industrialized capitalist mass production. Meanwhile, in Britain, successful manufacturers took the shortest route possible to becoming country gentlemen, a process eloquently described by Martin Wiener in his book *English Culture and the Decline of the Industrial Spirit 1850–1980* (1981). Wiener is American.

Ruskin's easy fit of industrialized progress with the prospect of perdition had been anticipated by another London eccentric, William Blake. From his dwelling in Hercules Road, Lambeth, Blake could see the famous Albion Mills on the banks of the Thames at Blackfriars. Built by Samuel Wyatt in 1786, Albion Mills employed rotary steam engines designed by Boulton & Watt (with gear trains by John Rennie). This amazingly advanced manufactory could produce 6,000 bushels of flour a week. Unfortunately, while it was a symbol of industrial progress, it also turned Lambeth into an ugly slum. When the mills were destroyed by fire in 1792, it was assumed that the culprits were Luddite arsonists.

As London's most singular industrial building, Albion Mills furnished Blake with his nightmare vision of Satanic ugliness conquering England's supposed pastoral idyll. London was to the poet a "human awful wonder

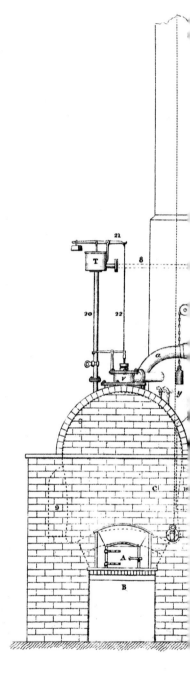

Farey, delin.

Right Technical drawing of 'Mr Watt's Patent Rotative Steam Engine' of 1787. With his partner Matthew Boulton, James Watt established a steam-engine factory in Birmingham's Soho in 1774. Engines became, to some critics, metaphors of horror. In particular, some were alarmed that the rotation of a piston somehow suggested the intromittent male sexual organ.

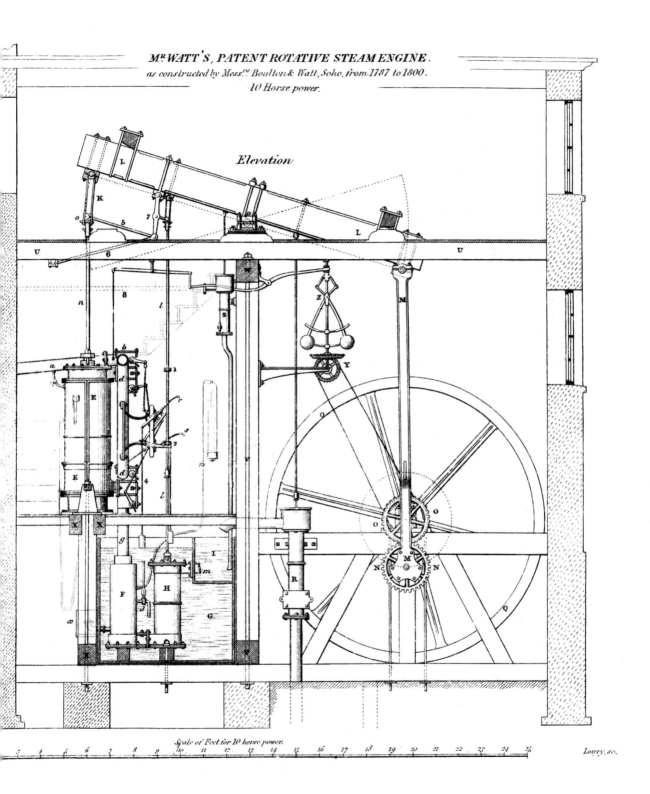

MR WATT'S, PATENT ROTATIVE STEAM ENGINE.

as constructed by Messrs. Boulton & Watt, Soho, from 1787 to 1800.

10 Horse power.

Elevation

Scale of Feet for 10 horse power:

Lowry, sc.

Left A. C. Pugin, *Fire in London* (1808). Albion Mills was visible from William Blake's bedroom in Hercules Road, Lambeth. This highly automated factory was a symbol of the industrial revolution's technical achievements, but it turned Lambeth into a slum. It was the inspiration for the poet's "dark Satanic mill".

of God". Just as beauty was an escape from ugliness, so ugliness itself seemed to be the price paid for commercial and industrial progress. The charred and ruined mills (which were never rebuilt) stood as a reprimand to vanity.

The human awful wonder of railways

Ruskin came to believe that every modern invention generates ugliness. Railways destroyed the countryside. New sports such as mountaineering turned the Alps into racecourses (sport was often used as a signifier of barbarianism). Although he became a utopian socialist after a period of crusty Tory bigotry, Ruskin believed that modern forms of collectivism (as opposed to the inevitable beauty that was the product of the work practices of the medieval guilds) would lead only to mass-produced ugliness. Socialism does not care for beauty. And everywhere the snigger of Mephistopheles, who has trapped us into this false bargain of wealth in exchange for ugliness, is barely disguised behind the hiss of industrial steam.

So it was Paradise Lost. Given the Freudian insights we can now exploit, the loss of beauty in nineteenth-century life created symptoms in public health similar to sexual hysteria or mental disease: apathy, despondence, cynical indifference and brutish behavior. According to Ouida, pen name of the purplish novelist Maria Louise Ramé, "The typical, notable creation of the iron beast's epoch… is the cad, vomited forth from every city and town in hundreds, thousands, millions". Just as sex was, in Hieronymus Bosch's world, an ugly expression of man's depraved nature, so in this torsioned vision of the 19th century, a proliferation of sexual adventurers was the sad and inevitable result of an ugly environment.

It is not difficult to read into Ruskin's critique of the fast-evolving modern world with its hateful machines some metaphors of frustration, perhaps of a sexual character. We will see that the steam piston, with its disturbing intromittent action that apes copulation, is especially vilified by Ruskin. The great critic shunned repellent sex and he also shunned repellent cities.

In this interpretation, beauty was ever more withdrawn from the public. The ugly sewing machine replaced the folklorique spinning wheel, and veneered, machine-made furniture replaced solid home-made oaken linen presses and hand-hewn Windsor chairs. In his *Academy Notes* of 1856, Ruskin explained that you knew the man in Holman Hunt's painting *The Awakening Conscience* (1853) was (here we go again) a cad or a sexual adventurer because of the "fatal newness" of the furniture. The new shiny brown piano was ugly but, to compound the offence, it also suggested that its owner was the social type who was later described as the sort of person who buys his own furniture.

Then there was not only the sexual licence and the ugly filth which the

Above *The Collier* aquatint by Robert Havell (1814), showing John Blenkinsop's 'Salamanca' on the Leeds-Middleton Railway in 1812, one of the very first images of a steam train from George Walker's *The Costume of Yorkshire* (1814). Like the sinister Albion Mills, Blenkinsop's rack locomotive was a technical triumph to some, but an ugly intrusion into nature to others.

Overleaf left Maria Louise Ramé used the pen name Ouida. Her novels include *Strathmore* (1865) and *Moths* (1880). Her overblown style never attracted critical admirers, but her commentary on High Victorian life is a gloss on middle-class anxieties about the modern manners and the uglification of contemporary life.

Overleaf right E. Wormser, Part of piston from Maudslay's machine, chromolithograph (1856). Henry Maudslay was a toolmaker working for Marc Isambard Brunel. Prints of his block-making machines and piston were sold in a portfolio, but were also available separately for the instruction of the masses. They were both a reprimand and an inspiration: industry created artificial beauty, while it destroyed the natural kind.

Machine Maudslay; Guide de la tige du Piston.

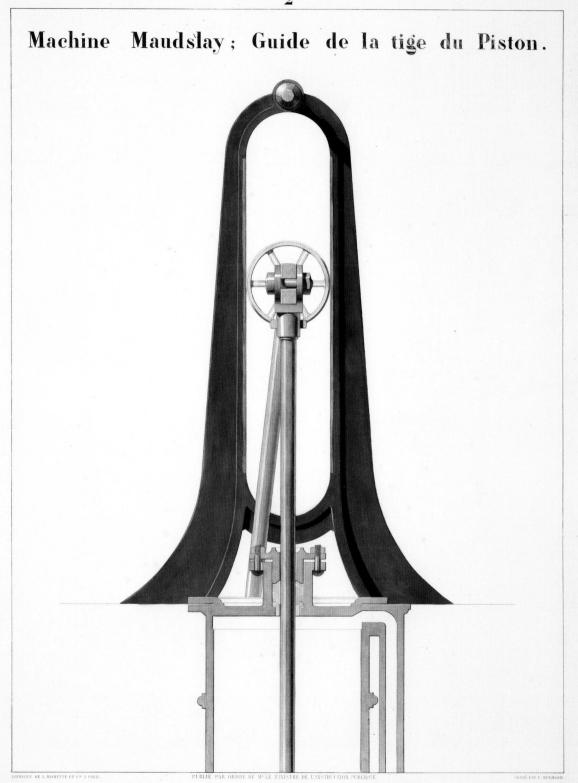

LIBRAIRIE DE L. HACHETTE ET Cⁱᵉ A PARIS.   PUBLIÉ PAR ORDRE DE Mʳ LE MINISTRE DE L'INSTRUCTION PUBLIQUE.   GRAVÉ PAR E. MORISSE.

10692. - THIRLMERE & HELVELLYN.

modern world generated in cities. There was also the ugly damage the same fruits of industry did to the virgin countryside. The railway was not seen as a safe and convenient mode of transport, but as a vicious device that disembowels mountains.

Ruskin wrote a preface to Robert Somervell's *A Protest Against the Extension of the Railways in the Lake District* (1876) which is a classic of rhetorical invective. It is also perfect evidence of his hatred of "the stupid herds of modern tourists", as well as evidence of his need to save the same stupid herds from descent into hellish ugliness.

The railway was planned to run from Windermere to Keswick. Ruskin sees the plan as a demonstration of "the frenzy of avarice". His favourite landscapes are going to be blasted into a treeless waste of ashes. Sheep will be driven from Helvellyn. All of Wales and Cumberland will be blown up into a heap of slate shingle. All this simply to find minerals and slate that offers only to roof all of England into "one vast Bedlam".

Of the educational benefits of rail travel Ruskin says, "What the new railway has to do is to shovel those who have come to Keswick, to Windermere – and to shovel those who have come to Windermere to Keswick". And in the course of this ludicrous process, noble Grasmere will become a cesspit and its beach a

Left A postcard view of Helvellyn and Thirlmere (c.1900), photomechanical print. John Ruskin was dismayed at the intrusion of the railway into his beloved Lake District: it was caused, he said, by a frenzy of avarice and would result only in the whole country becoming a vast Bedlam.

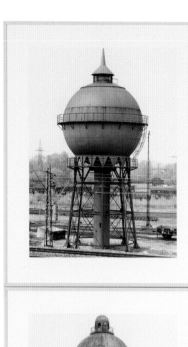

bitter landscape of broken ginger beer bottles. In another illustration of how sports and entertainments were considered ugly and demeaning, Ruskin envisaged the ultimate aesthetic horror of a steam merry-go-round defacing the Lake District.

From Derwentwater to Düsseldorf

Left Bernd and Hilla Becher, *Water Towers* (1980), gelatin silver print. The first generation of Modernists was infatuated by the beauty of simple machines. With great skill and a little irony, the Bechers beautified the confrontational ugliness of industrial infrastructure.

Overleaf Andreas Gursky, *Atlanta* (1996), chromogenic colour print. Gursky was a pupil of Bernd and Hilla Becher. He applies the same, cool, ironic, detached technique to his vast photographic commentaries.

Meanwhile, back in Ruskin's city, the sky is dark and polluted. People live in iron houses. The air is poisoned and the sky lacerated by wires carrying electricity generated by those same pistons slipping in and out of nameless, but huge, cylinders. Clean, efficient electricity was specially damnable to the romantic nineteenth-century imagination. Thoreau said bitterly "electricity kills darkness" while "candles illuminate it".

Like Bosch's own infernal landscapes, overgrown and diseased cities spread their scurvy. Life is waste, not leisure. Sanity is swapped for mania. Egotism and terror replace courage and generosity as influential human attributes. This theme of industrialisation and ugliness goes from Hogarth to Blake to Marx, Ruskin, Dickens, Poe, Zola and the Green Party.

We now see the remains of industry as hauntingly beautiful. Indeed, when Bernd and Hilla Becher began their photographic collaboration in 1959 their purpose was simply to record Germany's fast disappearing infrastructure. By the time of Bernd Becher's death in 2007, the couple were considered to be leading conceptual artists – not mere industrial archaeologists with a large-format camera.

Bernd Becher had studied painting at the Staatliche Akademie der Bildenden Künst in Stuttgart then typography at the Kunstakademie Düsseldorf. Dutifully photographing a rusting world of mineheads, gasometers, grain elevators, water towers, silos and warehouses, the Bechers often displayed their work in grids. The large-format camera with its rising front lens produced images where perspective is diminished and a haunting sense of unreality is established. They took delight in typology and morphology and the strangely beautiful patterns in the wreckage of the *Wirtschaftswunder*. Their book *Anonymous Structures: A Typology of Technical Construction* was published in 1970 and was an inspiration to their students, who included Thomas Ruff, Candida Höfer and Andreas Gursky. The last named is one of our great poets of industrial banality. What Ruskin thought ugly, the Bechers find beautiful. So do we.

5.

When Nature is Ugly, or Monument Valley and I-35

Who wrote the rule that nature is beautiful?
Why do we enjoy views?
Why do we enjoy cuteness?
Who said flowers are beautiful?

What could be more beautiful than mountain scenery? Quite a lot, actually.

The mountains which Ruskin and other Victorian sentimentalists worried to save from the ravages of the industrial world were not always popular. On the contrary, mountains used to represent a prospect of triply-distilled horror. And for very good reasons: the psychological revulsion against mountains was based on practical objections.

If you had no more sure a means of transport than feet or a horse, mountains represented not exhilarating freedom, great views, wildflowers and fresh air, but stifling confinement – with a measure of added danger. "Ugly" was not a word that an Occitan *paysan* of the fourteenth century would have used, but as he gazed, perhaps, on the Dentelles de Montmirail, if he gazed at them at all, his reaction would have been somewhere between disgust and fear.

The assumption of mountains into our vocabulary of the "beautiful" is a relatively recent one. Like public schools, Scottish national costume and morris dancing, mountains were an "invention" of the 19th century. It is one of the great symmetries of cultural history that the same people who were busy destroying nature were, at the same time, busy discovering it. The architect Viollet-le-Duc, for example, rather over-busily reinvented French medieval architecture – and was also a pioneer *alpiniste* so he can also be said to have reinvented French mountains.

Mont Ventoux is a 1,910m mountain 20km north-east of Carpentras. Since it rises above what is generally level scenery, rather separate from the main body of the Alps, it presents a forbidding aspect from afar. Nowadays, Mont Ventoux is one of the most fearsome *étapes* of the Tour de France. When the poet Petrarch climbed Mont Ventoux on 26 April 1336, he later claimed his purpose was to enjoy the view.

However, hyperventilating, perhaps, at the top and possibly discomfited by the attentions of the short-toed eagles and the maddening wind (*ventoux* means windy in the local dialect), Petrarch had a profound spiritual experience. On his return to level ground, he promptly wrote a now famous letter to the Augustinian monk, Dionigi di Borgo San Sepolcro. In this letter Petrarch claimed to be the very first person to have climbed a mountain for pleasure or instruction. Or at least, this conceit became conventional wisdom thanks to the poet's self-mythologizing which was accepted by Jakob Burckhardt (1818–97), the first modern historian of the Renaissance. Burckhardt reckoned Petrarch's ascent of Mont Ventoux to be the beginning

Above The second ascent of
Mont Blanc was made by Swiss
alpiniste, physicist and geologist
Horace Bénédict de Saussure
in 1788. Here he and his *équipe*
rest on the Grand Géant glacier.
The conquest of mountains
was a symbol of modern man's
subjugation of threat.

of a modern sensibility, which had an appreciation and an understanding of nature rather than a revulsion against it.

Busy researchers have now disproved Petrarch's claim to mountaineering originality. The Emperor Hadrian went up Etna in 121 to see the sunrise, and it seems a local man went up Ventoux a few years before 1336 – but Petrarch's claim was poetically accurate if not quite technically sound. Here for the first time the idea of a mountain as a frightful, ugly thing, a source of menace, threat and foreboding, was modified to the mountain as an object of veneration and a stimulus for rumination.

The dreadful depth of the precipice

Yet in the seventeenth century, the Alps were still seen as undigested deformed lumps. If they had a purpose at all, it was only as a horrible curtain protecting the "garden" of Italy from tourist herds originating up north. The ugly Alps were construed as a necessary dramatic anticipation of the beauties awaiting intrepid travellers further south. To enhance the pleasures, the horrors were necessary.

Here, in Italy the sun shone and Nature was genial and beneficent. Layers of history were so deep that it was said there were ruins piled upon ruins. Before the invention of the Picturesque, the state of mind which sees nature as a painting or a garden, all a traveller found in mountains was, philosophically speaking, a formless void. And, from the practical point of view, a place where you might very easily fall down a horrible precipice or meet not only a short-toed eagle, but a carnivorous animal or a malignant mountain spirit. Mountains gave no comfort to the eye. Mountains were ugly.

The poet John Milton visited Italy in 1638, 14 years before his blindness became disabling. He found mountains to be barren although he allowed that there might be a sort of craggy, precipitous pleasure to be had among them. Then in *The Indian Emperor* (1667), Dryden says: "High objects, it is true, attract the sight; but it looks up with pain on craggy rocks and barren mountains, and continues long on any object, which is wanting in shades of green to entertain it". Dryden still thought mountains ugly.

A traveller called John Dennis crossed the Alps in 1688 and left a marvellous account of the late seventeenth-century feeling for mountains: "The impending Rock that hung over us, the dreadful Depth of the Precipice, and the Torrent that roar'd at the Bottom, gave us such a view as was altogether new and amazing. On the other side of that Torrent, was a Mountain that Equall'd ours… Its craggy cliffs, which we half discerned thro' the misty Gloom of the Clouds that surrounded them, sometimes gave us a horrid Prospect. And sometimes its face appear'd smooth and Beautiful, as the most even and fruitful Vallies. So different from themselves were the different parts of it: in the same Place Nature was severe and Wanton. In the meantime we walk'd upon the very brink, in a literal sense, of Destruction. One stumble and both Life and Carcass had been at once destroyed. The sense of this produc'd different motives in me, viz. a delightful Horrour, a terrible Joy, and at the same time that I was infinitely pleas'd I trembled".

But by 1741 Richard Pococke, later the Protestant Bishop of Meath, made the first recreational visit to a glacier and the Alps soon became acceptable as a source of delight. The very brink of destruction had become a starting point for tourism. And by the 1780s, mountaineering was fast evolving as a sport with rules established by Horace-Bénédict de Saussure (who climbed Mont Blanc in 1787). The English were pioneers in this rediscovery: no longer fearful travellers through misty gloom, they turned the Alps into a playground for hearties. The Alpine Club was founded in London in 1857 and when the British climber Edward Whymper successfully scaled the forbidding Matterhorn in 1865, it was the beginning of the Golden Age of Mountaineering.

Bringing the once horrible mountains into the arena of recreation was one of the most remarkable achievements of the Industrial Age. And this process was completed at the moment of maximum economic activity in Britain. With the destruction of some areas of natural beauty by canals, railways, mills, factories, reservoirs, housing, gasworks, mines, poorhouses, crematoria, wharves, docks, asylums, hospitals, waterworks, quarries and storage facilities, compensation was sought for industrialization in the appropriation of nature's greatest spectacle as entertainment.

Opposite The Matterhorn was one of the last Alpine peaks to be conquered by man. Edward Whymper's "successful" attempt was made in 1865, although four of his companions died on the descent, as if confirming medieval fears and taboos.

Blank confusion

Mountains are just the largest example of changing interpretations of nature. Never mind that the same new buildings and institutions deplored by Ruskin and others have been energetically preserved from destruction by the Victorian Society since 1958; so far from alienating the public from beauty, industrialization just created new opportunities to appreciate it.

The moment when raw nature began to be most appreciated was the same moment that the word "ugly" begins to appear more often in the commentary of painters and poets. At the very beginning of the photographic era, the painter John Constable was among the first to see the world without benefit of the filters of art. He had a clear view on ugliness. This was that it did not exist in nature. "I never saw an ugly thing in my life, for let the form of an object be what it may – light, shade and perspective will always make it beautiful". Very well, but many of Constable's most famous paintings were not of uncontaminated rural idylls. His canvases of Suffolk

Above left/right Two magic
lantern slides of the Swiss Alps
(1925 and 1890s). The Matterhorn
railway was begun in 1888. The
invasion of the Alps by steam
locomotion offered commentators
two versions of horror: the
terrifying mountain itself plus the
subjugation of wild, uncontaminated
nature by a noisy, greasy, dirty
product of the industrial revolution.

Above John Constable's *Windmill Among Houses and Rainbow*, oil on paper (c.1800s). Constable's idyllic scenes of the English countryside were often images of industrialized agriculture.

A nineteenth-century windmill is no less an intrusion into Nature than a twenty-first century wind-turbine-generator.

canals and mills recorded the industrialisation of the countryside.

Wordsworth we know found beauty in daffodils, but he also found ugliness in the noise and chaos of Bartholomew Fair, last held in Islington in 1855. And in the poverty surrounding this thieves' market of lascivious and profoundly urban entertainments:

Oh, blank confusion! true epitome
Of what the mighty City is herself,
To thousands upon thousands of her sons,
Living amid the same perpetual whirl
Of trivial objects, melted and reduced
To one identity, by differences
That have no laws, no meaning and no end.

But Wordsworth also marks a beginning of the moment when poets began to find charm in the new city. His sonnet *Composed upon Westminster Bridge* asserts that a London sunrise, even if it be over workhouses and crematoria and seen though smog, is one of the most beautiful things imaginable. Already in the late 18th century George Crabbe and Oliver Goldsmith had begun to doubt the delights of rustic life in verse. Crabbe's *The Village* proposes an unsentimental realism about the hardships of life behind the plough. And Goldsmith speculates about the evacuees form his *Deserted Village* finding a new home in America, on the banks of the River Altamaha. This is somewhere between the cities we know today as Jacksonville, Florida, and Savannah, Georgia.

The question whether nature is always beautiful can only be answered if you have a concept of ugliness. As the Romantics presented the once loathed mountains as the perfect expression of natural beauty, so today the sandstone buttes of Monument Valley on the plateau of the Colorado River are presented as a Grail of North American tourism. And tourism is a construct which, generally, depends on the acquisition of

Above and opposite Magic lantern slide of Monument Valley in Utah (c.1900). As Dryden knew "High objects…attract the sight". The sandstone buttes of Monument Valley are 1000 feet above the valley floor. A symbol of uncontaminated nature, they have been in the background of several Hollywood movies, including John Ford's *Stagecoach* (1939), Dennis Hopper's *Easy Rider* (1969), and Ridley Scott's *Thelma and Louise* (1991).

beauty by those consuming it. Only a dull person would deny that the sensational Monument Valley is an exciting spectacle, but to another sensibility the serene symmetry and calm of the I-35 freeway (completed in 1971), which goes awesomely from Laredo, Texas, to Duluth, Minnesota, offers its aesthetic pleasures too. I-35's majestic purpose of connecting Canada to Mexico, its blacktop subordination of scrub, its confidence and clarity… these present a prospect not of industrial ugliness, but, perhaps, of great beauty.

Above The star-nosed mole, *condylura cistata*, is disturbing because it appears to lack a face.

Cute, fluffy creatures

The evolutionary argument that we find some creatures disagreeable because they excite prehistoric fears does not work. A cobra is not ugly. And, one imagines, a sabre-toothed tiger was a handsome, regal beast. On the other hand, there is some agreement that the star-nosed mole, a by no means threatening creature, is disturbingly difficult to look at. In 2010, *The New York Times* reported Nancy Kanwisher, a neuroscientist at the Massachusetts Institute of Technology, explaining that the mole was disturbing because it appeared to have no face.

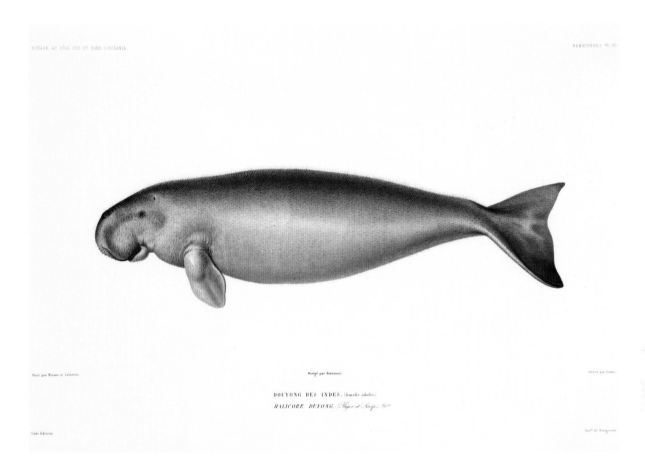

DOUYONG DES INDES. (femelle adulte)
HALICORE DUYONG. (Illiger et Geoff.) 1811.

Above Engraving by Oudet of a sea cow or halicore dugong, from French navigator Jules-Sébastien-César Dumont-Urville's *Voyage au Pole Sud et dans l'Oceanie* (1842–53). A categorical confusion, or wishful thinking, made many mariners mistake the ugly sea cow for a beautiful, sexualized mermaid.

There is some evidence that research biologists are more interested in animals which conform to accepted notions of beauty. An article in *Conservation Biology* in 2010 by Morgan J. Trimble analyzed the literature on about 2,000 South African species. One of them was the manatee, or sea cow. African natives believe manatees were once human, and perhaps this is the source of the categorical confusion that created the maritime delusion of the mermaid. Killing them is taboo. So the manatee might be an interesting cultural study. And there are scientific reasons to study manatees too: they show some ability to deal with tasks involving discrimination and have long-term memory. That's to say, they are unusually intelligent. However, it turns out that the manatee is "the least studied large mammal"… because it is fat and gross.

It is not true that the movement to anti-pastoral ideas begun by Crabbe and Goldsmith led directly to The Ugliest Dog in the World competition, but the latter is a powerful argument against too fond an idea that nature's fruits are always a cause of delight. This annual event in Petaluma, California, has been dominated in recent years by the Chinese Crested breed, distinguished by the hairlessness that is an incomplete dominant genetic trait. A recent winner not only had no hair, but only one eye and three legs.

Opposite The hairless Chinese
Crested dog regularly does well
in The Ugliest Dog in the World
Competition held annually in
Petaluma, California. One example
named Sam won in 2003, 2004
and 2005.

Above A bulldog winning the Ugly
Pet Contest held at Chicago Fair,
1984. In Stanley Coren's *The
Intelligence of Dogs* (1994), the
bulldog ranked 78th of the 80
breeds analyzed.

Flora's pornography

A revisionist view of nature has also been considered, and this may be
a surprise, by members of the Royal Horticultural Society which in 2009
voted to determine that the priapic and foul-smelling corpse flower
(*Amorphophallus titanum*) was the world's ugliest plant. The catalogue
of other ugly plants included bastard cobas (*Cyphostemma juttae*) from
Namibia, also known as the wild grape; birthworts (*Aristolochia gigantea*),
with a complex, umbilical intertwined stem: elephant's trunk (*Pachypodium
namaquanum*), also from Namibia and covered in spines; tree tumbo
(*Welwitschia mirabilis*), a living fossil from southern Africa; thorn of the
cross (*Colletia paradoxa*), a South American shrub; stinky squid (*Pseudocolus
fusiformis*), a mushroom discovered in Pittsburgh, 1915; sea onion (*Bowiea
volubilis*) looks like a nastily attenuated asparagus; and vegetable sheep
(*Raoulia eximia*), a hairy vegetable mound from New Zealand which can be
mistaken for the ovine sub-family of the goat-antelope *Bovidae* ruminants.

Any even-handed survey of this hideous collection of malodorous, deformed,
aggressive, unlovable punk flora would agree that, relative values
notwithstanding, nature is indeed capable of furnishing us with material
that is disturbing. Here is pornography, not erotica, on a stalk and in bud.
And, as a footnote of eccentric erudition, it is, perhaps, worth noting that
the word "smut" has horticultural origins. It actually means a fungal disease
of corn, rather than the moral problem of dirty pictures. The beauty of
diseased plants – and the fascination of dangerous or difficult ones – warns
us against glib answers to the question of natural beauty.

It was M. C. Cooke who wrote the memorably titled *Rust, Smut, Mildew
and Mould* (1865). It is a song of praise to fungus, directed at the newly
emerging market of amateur microscope owners who were busy exploring
the outer suburbs and countryside made available by the growth of the
railway network. There is something ineffably touching, and not to say
ineffably strange, about Arthur and Mabel putting the city behind them
and travelling to New Cross where they might enjoy "A stroll away from the
busy haunts of men… along the slopes of the railway cutting, we shall be
sure to find the plant called goatsbeard…[whose] leaves… present a
singular appearance, as if sprinkled with gold dust, or rather being deficient
in lustre, seeming as though some fairy folk had scattered over them a
shower of orange-coloured chrome or turmeric…"

Ford Madox Ford was born around the same time Arthur and Mabel were
clambering up railway cuttings looking for aesthetic weeds. In *England and
the English* (1907), he provides a nicely disdainful description of the countryside,
where he found a "…tremendous waste of plant life, the ownerless blades of
grass, the enormous spread of fields, the scampering profusion of wild rabbits,
or the unnumerable and uncontrolled sheep". What could be more beautiful
than a weedy railway embankment? I-35 for sure.

6. Kitsch, or The Intoxication of Bad Taste

Opposite Gebrüder Thonet's mass-produced *Model No. 14* chair (1859). Industrialised, flat-packed and universal, the original café chair was admired by Le Corbusier as the ultimate in elegant design.

Why is my taste better than yours?
When did shopping become competitive?
Who said fakes are ugly?
Why bother with rules?

The nineteenth century industrialized ugliness. Crimes of art were perpetrated with the same callous thoroughness of global warfare and greedy colonialism. Industry provided the means to mass produce beauty, or, at least, an agreed version of it, but on the available evidence… ugliness was preferred. What does this tell us about human motivation and, indeed, human perversity? Even in the twenty-first century, we are still struggling to come to terms with what industry has done to art and nature.

Put it this way: from the perspective of the early twenty-first century, the entire history of the previous century's design, at least the Authorized Version of the Modern Movement with two capital 'M's, can be seen as a call to order. It was an attempt to reinvent rules that were lost when pattern books were replaced by machine tools.

Industrialization created kitsch in two ways. For the first time in history it was possible to manufacture large numbers of anything without necessarily bothering with taste or refinement. Since the new consumers largely lacked education, taste and refinement were not really needed. Anything went. Production and consumption were no longer the privilege of an elite, but were opened up to all social classes. Somewhat depressingly, this led to generalized mediocracy rather than generalized excellence.

Industrial production did not just alienate workers, it alienated the products coming out of the factory gates. Mass-produced goods had a weird character that was neither fake nor authentic. Not true fakes because a biscuit tin stamped with a gothic moulding was not really pretending to be anything other than what it was. Which is to say hideous, ugly, redundant dross. Not really authentic because the concept of authenticity depends on notions of morality and honesty which were absent where the mass production of decorated tins was concerned.

This completely compromised the old values which had supported architecture and design. Aristocratic privilege and carefully evolved craft traditions used to support taste: until the nineteenth century, there was, generally speaking, not much dispute about what was good and bad, and what was beautiful and ugly. But when Boulton & Watt's diabolically efficient steam engine replaced calloused, skilled hands, standards of taste were exploded.

One result? In the middle of the nineteenth century it was perfectly possible for Thonet's mass-produced *Konsumstuhl nr* 14, the famous café chair, to be available for sale alongside J. H. Belter's nightmarishly overwrought furniture. Both were machine-made; the one is, at least to our

Above A pair of Rococo Revival chairs by John Henry Belter, New York, (c.1850). New York-based German cabinetmaker and designer J. H. Belter was an exact contemporary of Thonet. He also used industrial production techniques, but his designs were aimed at a clientele with a taste for more elaborate effects and finishes, specializing in rococo revival pieces.

eyes, simple and dignified. The other is inappropriately fussy. In 2009 the global chain Muji introduced a redesigned version of the Thonet chair to muted approval of professors of taste. To have introduced a redesign of anything by Belter would have been kitsch.

The mid-nineteenth century was, after all, the age when architects argued about a "battle of the styles". Buildings were not mass produced until a hundred years later, but the very idea that you could choose a building's design rather as you might choose an appliance or an ornament from the Marshall Field or Sears Roebuck mail-order catalogue was evidence that there was no agreed standard of taste.

Do you fancy goods?

At the same time, the vast output of industry somehow trivialized nature. Factories were busier than Mother Nature! The idea of these sooty factories actually consuming the countryside was a recurrent nightmare among Victorian thinkers. But industry consumed and trivialized nature in another way. Suddenly, there was a world of the appallingly named "fancy goods". No denomination of any category of human activity has ever, surely, been so depressingly inept as "fancy goods". And fancy goods often appropriated nature, not merely as a decorative motif, but in fragments. The fly in amber, the orchid in the bell-jar, the butterfly pinned to a board, the stuffed owl, the fern in the Wardian case, dioramas and the zoo – all are examples of a false control of nature. And they are all superlative examples of kitsch.

A good place to start looking for understanding, although there are very many alternatives, would be the astonishing collection of nineteenth-century glass paperweights that have been collected in the Bergstrom-Mahler Museum in Neenah, Wisconsin. The source of this collection was a personal passion of Evangeline Hoysradt, later Mrs Bergstrom, who found in a Florida antique fair in 1935 a glass paperweight that reminded her of a childhood favourite. By 1939, her collection was about 200 items and was exhibited at the very august Art Institute of Chicago. A sort of national hysteria followed. There were appearances on radio chat shows, a self-published monograph, and great celebrity in the weirdly competitive world of glass paperweights was acknowledged by the opening of the museum in Neenah in 1959.

The glass paperweight craze is thought to have begun when Pietro Bigaglia exhibited an example of his own high craft at the Vienna Fair in 1845. From Bigaglia on, paperweights represent in miniature the nineteenth-century attitude to design: at once marvels of industry, but also aesthetic horrors. Fancy goods, in fact. If the public had a morbid appetite for the marvellous, then the industrialists and entrepreneurs who manufactured paperweights were well able to stimulate and satisfy it.

Paperweights (and their close relatives, snow globes) often, as decorative motifs, use real scraps of nature. To have the plant and animal world subjugated to, indeed embedded in, an industrial process is magnificently emblematic of the skewed aesthetics of Victoriana. It was, to borrow the title of Celeste Olalquiaga's strange, ruminative and provocative 1999 book, an artificial kingdom. Paperweights containing fragments of seahorse were just the most popular example of nature's subjugation to industrial production. The aquarium, for example, became popular at the same moment. A commercially available "parlour aquarium" in the late 1850s included a submerged and miniature Alpine mountainscape to amuse the fish and the spectators. This attachment to nature in miniature (collecting sea shells and

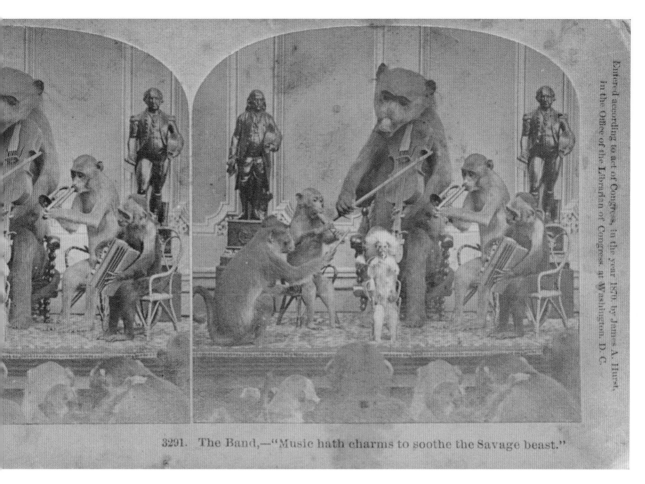

3291.   The Band,—"Music hath charms to soothe the Savage beast."

Above Stuffed monkeys playing musical instruments. The ingenuity and technical genius on display at the 1851 Great Exhibition was exactly matched by the volume of brainless, lowering kitsch on offer. Many of these fancy goods involved anthropomorphised taxidermy "aping" human activities.

Overleaf left and right A Victorian stuffed owl and a modern glass paperweight. This category of object which almost always resists the imposition of "good" design.

Left A fern house at Kew Gardens. "Pteridomania", the collection of ferns, was a Victorian fad. The amateur botanist and collector Dr Nathaniel Bagshaw Ward developed the protective glass "Wardian" case in 1829. Intended to protect his herb collection from London's vicious pollution, it was a metaphor of the Victorian ideal of "devices to suppress and contain Nature".

butterflies were other popular activities) produced not only an abundance of goods and containers that we would classify as kitsch, but is at the same time touching evidence of a popular need to escape from industrialized ugliness – even while encouraging it.

Pteridomania was the craze for fern-collecting, a sort of collective madness that was so intense in Britain that it crossed all social classes and led to the alarming depletion of various fern varieties in the Highlands of Scotland and Wales. The term we probably owe to Charles Kingsley, and it appears in his book *Glaucus; or, The Wonders of the Shore* (1855), but dates back two decades earlier when the new railways made out-of-town excursions a possibility for amateur botanists.

Kingsley writes of pteridomania: "Your daughters, perhaps, have been seized with the offending Pteridomania… and wrangling over unpronounceable names of species… and yet you cannot deny that they find enjoyment in it, and are more active, more cheerful, more self-forgetful over it than they would have been over novels and gossip, crochet and Berlin-wool".

And, in connection with the need to put everything on display, ferns were often housed in decorated glass containers – known as Wardian Cases – designed by Dr Nathaniel Bagshaw Ward and described in the pteridomanic best-seller, *On the Growth of Plants in Closely Glazed Cases* (1842).

The Barnum & Bailey Greatest Show on Earth

THE PEERLESS PRODIGIES OF PHYSICAL PHENOMENA
AND GREAT PRESENTATION OF MARVELOUS LIVING HUMAN CURIOSITIES.

THE WORLD'S LARGEST, GRANDEST, BEST AMUSEMENT INSTITUTION.

Above Barnum & Bailey's circus specialized in 'peerless prodigies, human curiosities and physical phenomena,' all of which are advertised on this 1899 poster, printed by the Strobridge Litho. Co. (Cin'ti & New York). Freaks of nature may not be beautiful, but were a popular visitor attraction. Ugliness can give rise to a delicious thrill of pleasure.

And to continue the metaphor, the same age which saw the growth of museums – where everything was labelled and put on display – was also the age of the first modern shops where everything was also put on display. Both have an uneasy relationship to circuses and freak shows where everything odd was put on display. In Phineas T. Barnum's circus of 1842 there was, for example, an ugly fake mermaid comprising the upper part of an ape and the tail of a genus of the salmon family. Barnum also created beauty pageants and exploited ugly freaks of nature, including the original Siamese Twins Chang and Eng Bunker and Colonel Tom Thumb, the military dwarf. Barnum's kitsch, it needs to be said by those vigilant about the purity of scholarship and the exalting nature of beauty, fed directly into the system of US natural history museums.

Tasteless mass rubbish

The new department stores and the new Parisian arcades, such as the Passage Choiseul (1823–25) or the Passage Jouffroy (1847), were laboratories of kitsch for the new consumers. The 1851 Great Exhibition in London was,

itself, housed in a vast glass container like a Wardian case. A visitor to Crystal Palace might find, say, one of Hermann Ploucquet of Stuttgart's *tableaux vivants* (or rather, *morts*) of stuffed animals. There was, for example, a shockingly ugly Ermines' Tea Party, where the hideous animals were posed to strike the "attitudes, habits and occupations of rational creatures". The use of "rational" in that description can surely bear very little analysis. Taxidermy is in itself worthy of full-length study in the psychology of the nineteenth century. Alas, few enthusiasts are demented enough to have the stomach for such an enquiry.

The realist novelist Emile Zola was fascinated by shops and what they meant. He called his satire on consumerism, inspired by the Bon Marché department store in Paris, *Au Bonheur des Dames*. In one such arcade Zola's Nana in his 1880 novel of the same name was delighted by rubbish (which is to say fancy goods), including requisites in walnut shells, a Vendôme column containing a thermometer, fake jewels, gilded zinc and items made of cardboard that faked leather.

This profusion of ugliness was a great stimulus to art and design education, beginning in Britain, where industrialization had occurred first; then in Germany, which closely followed. The classic definition of kitsch is that of Gustav E. Pazaurek, a museum curator, poet, playwright and leading figure in the Deutscher Werkbund – an industrial collective intent on improving standards of design. We shall meet Pazaurek again in Chapter 9, but for now here is his view of the subject, as published in his paper "Good and Bad Taste in Applied Arts" (1912):

"The absolute antithesis of artistically inspired work of quality is tasteless mass rubbish, or kitsch: it disregards all the demands of ethics, logic and aesthetics; it is indifferent to all crimes and offences against material,

Above Joseph Paxton's "Crystal Palace" (the name was an ironic invention of contemporary journalism) was a giant Wardian case. Ruskin was dismayed. He said "We may… bridge the Bristol Channel with iron, roof the county of Middlesex with crystal and yet not possess one Milton or Michelangelo".

Opposite Showroom of the Wiener Werkstätte (or Vienna Workshop, a visual arts collective) in the "Austrian Building" at the Deutscher Werkbund exhibition, Cologne (1914). The room was designed by Josef Hoffmann and Eduard Josef Wimmer-Wisgrill. This exhibition was one of the first demonstrations of the beauty the Modern Movement believed it could achieve, and was greatly influential on an international scale, paving the way for industrial designers and artists. It was prematurely closed down with the outbreak of World War I.

technique, and functional or artistic form; it knows only one commandment: the object must be cheap and yet still attempt to create at least some impression of a higher value.'

Kitsch is not simply bad taste, although there is nothing "simple" about that tantalizingly difficult concept. In Pazaurek's definition, "kitsch" is the rubbish and tat of fancy goods which are brainlessly manufactured and brainlessly consumed. Kitsch is what we need art education to extirpate. Pazaurek and the Deutscher Werkbund's initiatives, not to say brain-washing, were a significant influence on the educational philosophy of the Bauhaus. The purpose of this most influential art school was, to put it simply, to tidy up the mess left by the nineteenth century.

In this campaign for industrialized beauty, ugly fancy goods were to be replaced by un-fancy ones. Curlicues out, right angles in. Ornament was crime. Purity was virtue. Dictators of left and right both enjoy kitsch, as Hellmut Lehmann-Haupt explained in his great study *Art under a Dictatorship*: there is a book waiting to be written that connects Stalin, Hitler, Mao, Idi Amin, Saddam Hussein, Kim Jong-il and Colonel Gaddafi. Indeed, it may be true that decaying civilizations produce kitsch and this would not be a very

Clockwise from top left Dictator taste, Idi Amin's house in Kampala (1979), Adolf Hitler with Eva Braun at Berchtesgarten (c.1935), Josef Stalin with daughter Svetlana (1937), and Sergeant Craig Zentkovich of 1st Brigade Combat Team photographs Saddam Hussein's pink bedroom in Baghdad (2003).

edifying book to read, even if it were one of powerful moral imperative. With dictators of one sort or another in mind, Hermann Broch in *Kitsch* (1933), contrasted ethics with aesthetics. 'The producer of kitsch,' he writes, 'must be judged as a contemptible being.' The consumer of Modernism was, by contrast, admirably well informed and the possessor of timelessly beautiful objects and furniture. Or so the theory went.

By some point in the mid-twentieth century, the revolutionary programme of the Bauhaus had won general acceptance, at least among a certain privileged caste of liberal, educated aesthetes. It had, indeed, with maximum absurdity, become the clean-edged orthodoxy of corporate culture. Witness Bauhaus furniture lined up like Panzers in the lobby and executive suite of, say, the CBS Building on Park Avenue in New York. It was at this point that kitsch leapt the species barrier.

No longer a term of condemnation for the cynical rubbish bought by uneducated consumers, kitsch was reinvented by a knowing elite, fatigued with the triumph of good manners represented by the "triumph" of the Modern movement. It was one front of the Uglification campaign that preoccupied opinion-formers in the arts at mid-century. By the time Gillo Dorfles's *Kitsch* was published in 1968, it had been elevated to what, just two years later, Tom Wolfe called "radical chic". It was cool to enjoy and promote ugliness.

Dorfles's influential book was sub-titled *An Anthology of Bad Taste*. Bernard Berenson declared that taste begins when appetite is gratified and the generation that re-uptook kitsch had been utterly sated on Modern movement politeness. A new generation admired what they self-consciously thought was bad. They agreed with Charles Baudelaire that bad taste was "intoxicating" because it suggested the aristocratic authority of not having to please.

Kitsch is the artful, knowing and sly elevation of bad taste, but aspects of its shifting definition reveal some absolutes about ugliness. Someone once said it's the corpse that's left when anger goes out of art. Death is often cited in definitions of kitsch: Celeste Olalquiaga says, "Kitsch is dead from the moment it is born," rather like Beckett's "birth was the death of him". To Clement Greenberg, kitsch is all about "vicarious experience and faked sensations… the epitome of all that is spurious". In this definition the Boboli Gardens with its strange confections of architecture and sculpture might be kitsch. Holy writ? Andy Warhol published his *Philosophy of Andy Warhol* in 1975. "The most beautiful thing in Tokyo is McDonald's".

The etymology of the word "kitsch" is instructive. It may be from early tourists to Europe wanting a "sketch" as a souvenir, but that's speculative. It has been said that it might be onomatopoeia for the sound of a Kodak shutter, a remembrance of a tourist capturing a sight for later vicarious enjoyment. More certain is that the German word *verkitschen* means to knock something off. To make a facsimile. Perhaps the earliest use in the contemporary sense – in that there was a level of approval as well as a level

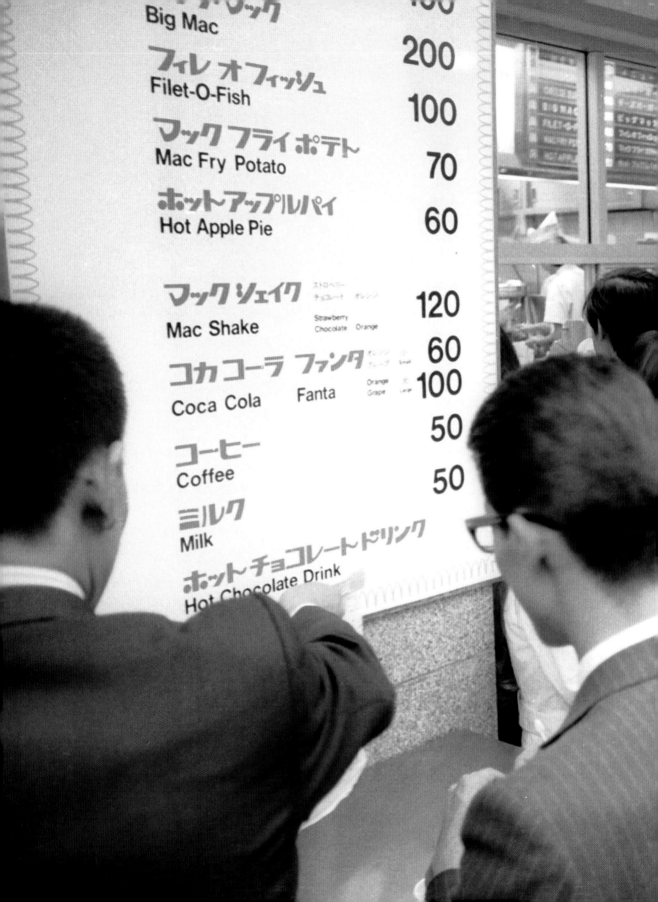

Above Morris Lapidus's Fontainebleau Hotel, Miami (1954). The commission was for "French provincial", but the architect went for what he called "wild and woolly modern with woggles". Grottoes and internal waterfalls were impressive features, as was a hydraulic dancefloor: a gold-standard kitsch classic. Weirdly, in his early career Lapidus was known for his Modernist tendencies, but later said "I thought Mies van der Rohe was an idiot. 'Less is more'? How stupid can you be. Less is not more. Less is nothing".

of condemnation – was by essayist Walter Benjamin who published in 1927 a rumination on the Surrealists which included the term *Traumkitsch*. Mingled here are ideas of dreaming and consumerism.

The flight of ducks

The lasting definition of kitsch is that it offers a facsimile experience. It apes the effect of art without bothering with the art itself. Kitsch aims for a crude immediacy. Kitsch goes straight for the response, not the intermediary aesthetic effect. Which takes us straight to Morris Lapidus's Fontainebleau Hotel, the largest establishment on Miami Beach when it opened in 1954 (the year before the essentially similar Disneyland). "Everyone will feel like he is being carried around on his own little silver platter," a spokesman announced. As Lapidus told *The New Yorker*, "Step inside the door and zingo! Euphoria". As the *Miami Herald* asked, "Gigantic? There must be a bigger word".

Lapidus was commissioned to design in "the French provincial" style, which had much excited the wife of Ben Novack, the developer, when on a European holiday. He liked to describe his work as "wild and woolly modern" and he specialized in shapes he called "woggles", which were apertures cut into buildings reminiscent of the holes found in Emmental cheese.

The excesses of the Fontainebleau are hilariously described by Jane and Michael Stern in their *Encyclopedia of Bad Taste* (1990). A dining room for 800 with a hydraulically controlled dance floor. Tons of red velour (in this, a 14-storey concrete structure); gilt fake rococo mirrors; gilt real European antiques. The restaurant was often animated by a *flambé* parade. It hosted the first Miss Universe contest and the moment he was demobbed in 1960, Elvis Presley made it his first stop. It had a grotto and lagoon.

Grottos and lagoons, along with the aroma of death and the certain presence of fakery, are almost compulsory in definitions of kitsch. The Fontainebleau Miami may represent the Gold Standard of twentieth century kitsch, but it has direct links to history. Morris Lapidus was concerned with theatre, illusion, grossness, impressiveness, postures and fake effects. These you find in the Venus Grotto and subterranean lake which feature in "Mad" King Ludwig of Bavaria's Schloss Linderhof near Oberammergau.

Ludwig saw himself as a sort of fake Louis XIV and Linderhof, which includes a Hall of Mirrors, was his Versailles, although a little smaller. His bedroom faced north because, in contraposition to *le Roi Soleil*, Ludwig styled himself the Night King. And across the waters of his subterranean grotto he enjoyed being rowed in his boat modelled on a golden swan. Twenty-four electric motors provided the power to illuminate electric lights, which rivalled in every way the Blue Grotto of Capri. But kitsch does not have to include grand gestures. Just as Elvis was getting out of his military khakis and into a Hawaiian shirt on Miami Beach, so *Coronation Street* was going on air in Britain.

Above left/right Ludwig II of
Bavaria's palace, Schloss
Linderhof, and its lavishly
decorated interior. "Mad" Kind
Ludwig's palace was completed in
1886. Like the Fontainebleau
Hotel, grottoes featured heavily.
The Venus Grotto was an
illustration of the first act of
Tannhauser, the King being
Richard Wagner's patron. The king
took his breakfast in a tree house
on the estate.

Overleaf The *Venusgrotte* at the
Schloss Linderhof. King Ludwig
would sail around the gaudily
decorated grotto in a specially
made boat.

Here is the long-suspected link between Elvis and the flying duck. When the series began in 1960, Elsie Tanner had a flying duck trio in her house at 11 Coronation Street. Flying ducks were an element of Hilda Ogden's "murial" at number 13. The ducks are used in sponsorship ads for Harvey's: The Furniture Store, and when a special edition of *Monopoly* was launched in 2000 to celebrate the 40th anniversary of the show, flying ducks were among the icons on the board along with Ena's hairnet, Bet's earrings and Betty's hotpot.

Another often photographed repository of de luxe kitsch is the Madonna Inn, San Luis Obispo. A visit was described by Umberto Eco in *Faith in Fakes* (1976). Eco noted the Jell-O colours, admired the William Tell Room, baroque cherubs, mother-of-pearl basins, toilets with Altamira details, Byzantine columns, Tyrolean-style pointers and references to Carmen Miranda, d'Annunzio, Liza Minnelli, LSD, Gaudí and Albert Speer. Amateurs of kitsch might also want to visit Dollywood, Dolly Parton's Great Smoky Mountain Family Amusement Park set in a lush 125 acres near Pigeon Forge, Tennessee. There is a Pinocchio theme park in Pistoia. On my very first visit to Padua, to see the Giotto murals in the Capella Arena, the starting point of Renaissance art, I noticed that Donald Duck's profile had been planted in flowers on a traffic roundabout.

Above Flying ducks became for mid-twentieth century aesthetes the perfect symbol of deplorable lower-class taste. The industrially-produced ducks have their conceptual origin in the first generation of decorative junk that appeared in the nineteenth century.

Opposite and overleaf The Madonna Inn, San Luis Obispo, is a commitment to excess. Established in 1958, burnt down in 1966, the Madonna family remained determined to astonish with the rebuild. The rooms are all romantically themed and have names like Yahoo, Cloud Nine and Jungle Rock.

Nearer home, any London souvenir stall is a perfect vernacular museum of kitsch so artless and inept that Zola's Nana would have been as intoxicated as Charles Baudelaire was on most weekday afternoons. Soft toys of indeterminate animal origin with Union Jack clothing. Novelty T-shirts. A plastic gilt Big Ben made in China: merely to describe is to condemn without having to recourse to critical bravura or analytical methodologies.

In 2009 the distinguished interior designer Jon Wealleans put on an exhibition of his paintings at London's Francis Kyle Gallery. Wealleans enjoyed the play on words between kitsch and kitchen, and meticulously depicted draining board clutter with a neutral eye and a steady hand plus an alarming preference for difficult Day-Glo colours. In their searing hideousness, submission to queasy effect and dumb noise, Wealleans's extraordinary paintings are a case study of self-conscious kitsch in the service of really rather disturbing ugliness. All the elements are there.

It can be funny. A (partial) account of the contents page of the Sterns' encyclopedia of bad taste provides an authoritative gloss on contemporary kitsch and makes hilarious reading in itself. Aerosol Cheese, Ant Farms, Artificial Grass, Artistry in Denim, Body Building, Breasts (enormous),

Above left Charles Baudelaire in 1855. The poet explained that the "pleasure of ugliness... is a thirst for the unknown and a taste for the horrible".

Above right A London souvenir stall. The Marxist historian Eric Hobsbawm has said that the less educated the population, the more likely it is to enjoy ornament.

Above The Troll, created by a Danish woodcutter and fisherman called Thomas Dam in 1959, tested several aesthetic assumptions. A doll modelled on neoclassical concepts of beauty would very likely have been much less popular.

Candle Art, Cedar Souvenirs, Chihuahuas, Christmas Trees (artificial), Day-Glo, Dinosaur Parks, Driftwood, Elvisiana, Fake Fur, Feminine Hygiene Spray, Fingernail Extremism, Fish Sticks, Fuzzy Dice, Gags and Novelties, Hawaiian Shirts, Hellenic Diners, Jogging Suits, Las Vegas, Lawn Ornaments, Lesiure Suits, Leopard Skin, Liberace, Limousines, Loud Ties, Macramé, Malls, Maraschino Cherries, Meat Snack Foods, Miniature Golf, Mobile Homes, Nehru Jackets, Nodding-head Dolls, Novelty Wrestling, Panty-hose Crafts, Dolly Parton (see above), Pepper Mills (huge), Pet Clothing, Polyester, Polynesian Foods, Poodles, Reclining Chairs, Shag Rugs, Snow Globes, Spam, Surf 'n' Turf, Tattoos, Taxidermy, Troll Dolls, Tupperware, Unicorns and Rainbows, Velvet Paintings, Wax Museums and White Lipstick.

And why is all this ugly? It goes straight back to Pazaurek's Principles.

7. Rubbish or The Zen of Crap

Opposite New York street scene (c.1900). Manhattan's streets in the early twentieth century were rubbish dumps and open sewers. Every horse would expel about 20lbs of excrement daily. The same horse would drink about 25 gallons of water, not all of it evaporating as sweat.

How can ugliness be inspiring?
Does poverty inhibit beauty?
Can utopia be designed?

We sentimentalize the past. This is a human default so familiar that we're inclined to describe it as "natural"… except it would be foolish to do so. It's not natural: it's artificial. Our view of the past is a work of art as contrived as an altarpiece or a symphony or a three-minute pop ditty.

People often assume that things used to be somehow better than they are today. And one part of that assumption is that today's cities are engines of filth and contamination, pushing out organophosphate toxins and poisoning citizens with lead particulates so that, unless we return to an imaginary unspoiled nature, we risk acquiring a portfolio of dire neuropsychiatric disorders, plus wrist-drop, foot-drop, delirium, palsy and coma.

But wait. In 1900 it is estimated that there were about 100,000 horses working on Manhattan. And these horses did not have dedicated flushing lavatories nor strict personal hygiene regimes, the latter a shortcoming also shared by many human New Yorkers of the day. Each horse produced about 20lbs of excrement every 24 hours. And since a horse will drink up to 25 gallons of water a day in hot weather and not all of it evaporates as sweat, it was not just solid excrement that perfumed the avenues and the cross streets.

And people piled their rubbish on the sidewalk so gutters were filthy. There was also the question of "night soil", an elegant evasion of faecal reality. The commercial underarm deodorant called *Mum* went to market in 1888, but was by no means universally adopted by the turn of the century. New York in 1900 was full of rubbish and stank. By comparison, today's Manhattan is as fragrant as a breeze-filled tuberose workshop in Grasse. Which was better?

The quality and aspirations of entire cultures may be judged both by the rubbish they produce and their attitude to it. Maybe it takes a very specialized aesthetic to see great beauty in the sanitation service compactor truck, grinding its way through the smelly contents of 96-gallon wheelie bins on its weekly urban cycle to return empty packs of Cheerios to a version of nature – but the mechanical ballet would have enthralled, say, Cicero or Goethe. Rubbish is not, as it were, to be dismissed. Rubbish can be divine. Or, at least, diabolically interesting.

Jesus and landfill

There is a relationship between our conception of rubbish, our conception of ugliness and visions of Hell that go back, quite literally, to Biblical times. These connections perhaps reveal a structure in the mind which

Above A view of Manhattan from Brooklyn, 1900s. The stink of the river, the sewage and the animals in the streets of late nineteenth century cities would have been unbelievable.

Above James Tissot, *Ancient Tombs, Valley of Hinnom*, pen and ink on paper, (c.1886). In Biblical times Gehenna was thought to be the entrance to Hell, but was actually a smouldering rubbish dump. Its apocalyptic qualities were noticed by both Jesus and John Milton.

Overleaf Landfill is the ultimate result of industrialized consumerism. The very first appeared at Champaign, Illinois in 1904. Rubbish is worth about $100 per ton.

predates the convictions and prejudices formed there by the acquired learning of culture. Waste and dirt may be "natural", but they are also instinctively repulsive.

Jesus knew about rubbish and used it as an admonition, as a symbol. In the Synoptic Gospels, Jesus mentions Gehenna by name II times. Gehenna is the Valley of Hinnom just south of Jerusalem. Originally the site of child sacrifices to the god Molech, Gehenna – foetid and dangerous – came to be considered an anteroom of Hell. It was not the place the dead were received – it was a place of punishment for the wicked. And the Islamic concept of Hell, Jahannam, is derived directly from it.

But the Valley of Hinnom was not Hell – it was a rubbish dump. Here dead animals, criminal corpses and waste were deposited. Just like a landfill in Essex or New Jersey, the Biblical Valley of Hinnom smouldered. Although in more resonant Biblical language, people assumed that Gehenna was not composed of rotting biomatter, but consumed by eternal fire. For Jesus it was a spectacle full of dire warning. John Milton picked up on this and wrote, "black Gehenna call'd, the type of Hell". And if rubbish has such power, it must have meaning as well.

It is possible to find a curious beauty, at any rate a fascination, with rubbish. At the University of Tucson, the archaeologist William Rathje has introduced his students to the new discipline of garbology. This is the haruspicy of rubbish. Students and researchers trawl through detritus in search of meaning. They can interpret milk cartons the way more conventional archaeologists interpret pottery shards or flint arrowheads. Rathje's Garbage Project has established a methodology for its discipline. Evidence is deep frozen before analysis, the better to facilitate scrutiny and maintain a modicum of health-protecting sanitary standards.

The whole theory and practice of waste has a certain weird beauty. Take landfill. With roots in Gehenna, it became a distinctively twentieth-century phenomenon, a frank demonstration of the hellish ugliness which social and art critics of the nineteenth century so fearfully predicted as the result of industrialization. Naturally, great expertise in landfill was developed in the US. Experts debate the question, but the very first was perhaps at Champaign, Illinois in 1904. This was followed two years later by Dayton, Ohio. And, as with so many things, the Second World War provided a special stimulus. To dispose of unwanted AFBs and barracks after 1945, the Army Corps of Engineers became expert at landfill.

Gehenna horrified, but the Fresh Kills landfill on Staten Island in New York, once the biggest in the world, has a mesmerizing quality that tempts suggestions about beauty. Brian Hayes, author of a majestic book entitled *Infrastructure* (2005), writes:

"Up close, what attracts the eye are those things that glint in the sun or flutter in the wind… what I noticed most was magnetic recording tape,

both the narrow audio kind and the wider ribbons of videotape; it was tangled in all the equipment, blowing across the surfaces of the landfill and decorating the fences like tinsel on a Christmas tree… [And the smell?] If it were a wine, I would describe it as fruity, sour, grassy, a little overripe".

That was in the Nineties; now the flutter of magnetic tape has been replaced by the more complex iridescence of CDs and the tragedy of computers, once so intelligent… now dumb. Landfills are the ruins of consumerism with all the poetry and elegy that implies.

A landfill site has an aesthetic quality for those prepared to see it and there are some who can and do. It is not just a static hole full of filth – it is a dynamic bioreactor. To prove that the study of rubbish is a discipline, critical terms have been adopted to facilitate discourse among experts, more sophisticated still than the emerging discipline of garbology. Sanitation specialists distinguish between trash which is dry and garbage which is wet. Then there is MSW, or municipal solid waste. Here is RDF or Refuse Derived Fuel. You dig the hole and then line it with a geotextile membrane. Layers of MSW are added daily and every day they are also covered with soil. A disagreeably named fluid called "leachate" may be developed by the rotting elements in the landfill, but this can be cycled through the system to retain a level of putrid activity.

When full, landfill is capped and reclaimed. Conventionally regarded as eyesores, the balletic movement of backhoe loaders and the sublime logic of the waste-to-energy equation make landfills things of odd beauty. Rubbish has an economic value as well. It is worth up to $100 a ton. This is the price someone will pay to have it taken away: there is a curious negative intelligence about the beautiful business of waste. There is truly a Zen quality about piles of crap.

Waste is a by-product of life just as litter and pollution are by-products of cities, so it is reasonable to be positive about them. But sometimes, perhaps often, straitened circumstances create beauty. Norman Lewis noticed this while travelling through Andalucia: poverty and misery positively encouraged the agreeable and uncluttered style of the *pueblos blancos*. Here is a rule trying to escape from an observation. "In poor times," Martin Heidegger wrote, "the poet is very rich". But sometimes straitened circumstances produce ugly circumstances. What's the difference?

An imbecile air of domination

Ruskin believed that "absolute and entire ugliness is rare", although this did not stop him being very concerned that he was going to be completely mired in it very soon. This may seem just one example of his maddening inconsistencies, but the sense of the observation is true. Once you start searching for it, once you try to isolate and define it, ugliness becomes almost as evanescent and as elusive as beauty. The more you bother to think about it, the more convinced you may

Above William Butterfield, Keble College, Oxford (1870). Designed as an advertisement for the Catholic Oxford Movement, Keble's strident red-brick deliberately contrasted with the familiar serene and honey-coloured Cotswold stone of Oxford. Its jagged polychrome Gothic Revival style led many to presume it had been designed by Ruskin, the Gothic champion.

become that definitions of ugliness depend not on the surface of things, but on their philosophical substance.

Given his strident views, it is poetic that Ruskin himself became associated with incorporated ugliness. When Kenneth Clark was writing his elegant and pioneering study, *The Gothic Revival*, in the early part of 1927, he noted that it was a common opinion of the day that Keble College, Oxford, was designed by Ruskin. And it was an equally common belief that it was the ugliest building on Earth. However, its actual architect was William Butterfield. He designed Keble in the style of eye-watering polychrome brick known as "Holy Zebra". This was a very self-conscious sort of Victorian corporate identity campaign, intended to advertise the confrontational postures of the Tractarians. (In the debate on the metaphysics of ugliness and Keble's place in that argument, it is irresistible to note that the College Chapel was sponsored by William Gibbs, who made his fortune from the commercialization of bird droppings collected in Peru.)

In the matter of confrontation, Ruskin had much to say in favour of

Butterfield's assertive architectural style. Of All Saints Margaret Street in London, he wrote, "It is the first piece of architecture I have seen… free from all signs of timidity or incapacity… it challenges fearless comparison with the noblest work of any time". The same freedom from timidity made the contemporary Albert Memorial another test for taste. Strolling around Kensington Gardens, the philosopher R. G. Collingwood found Scott's soulful tribute to a dead prince "visibly misshapen, corrupt, crawling, [and] verminous".

Perhaps this excess of positives makes a building ugly. So what exactly makes an entire city repellent? In his elegant and thoughtful travel book *Journey to Kars* (1984), Philip Glazebrook has a long and striking passage about the feeling of unease he experienced when visiting the Turkish town of Konya. Layard and Mitford had felt it too on one of their archaeological excursions. At the time of Glazebrook's visit, there was an outbreak of violent Islamism and a disturbing military presence which may have had an unsettling effect, but something less obvious than a clattering military helicopter or angry mujahideen made Konya ugly. Glazebrook found it was temporary and heartless and alien. It lacked oriental mystery. Thus he fell to wondering if our reaction to places is direct or associational. Are we repelled by things or by ideas?

Perhaps because it is so obviously a focus of conflicting cultures with their differing aesthetics, old and new economies with their disparate priorities and collisions of ethnicity, Turkey has often excited comment about the encroachment of modern ugliness upon a presumed state of more ancient and innocent beauty. Turkey badly influenced an earlier and much more affected writer, the orientalist-eroticist Pierre Loti. He says, in a pained lament about the insensitivity of contemporary life, that the Bosphorus has been destroyed by "idiotic speculators". Loti writes in 1900: "The exquisite Anatoli Hussar is disfigured by an American college, of a sinister ugliness, which has stuck itself above the ancient castle with an imbecile air of domination". Wistful of the past, he continues: "Frightful new buildings cumber the ground and factory chimneys rise besides minarets of which they are the miserable caricatures".

Turkey established and has continued something of a tradition in the creation of epic urban and suburban ugliness. Today, TOKÍ is the state-owned housing agency faced with a massive influx of urban poor into cities with no accommodation to cope. (The population of Istanbul has risen from less than two million in 1960 to over 12 million by 2009.) As a result, tower blocks of cruel banality have been erected in 81 cities. They use the same design, irrespective of location. Standardized low-rise villages have appeared, disfiguring the remote Kaçkar Mountains in the north east of the country.

Utopia, dystopia and cacotopia

The idea of utopia we owe to Thomas More and the idea of something less attractive, dystopia, we owe to John Stuart Mill. Cacotopia we owe to Jeremy Bentham. Many, like Bentham, misinterpreted More's utopia (meaning "no place") as eutopia ("good place"), due to their identical pronunciation. Cacotopia is a place where all is bad, or anti-utopia.

Our versions of dystopia and cacotopia continuously reveal our prejudices about beauty and our fears of ugliness's possible dominion over it. Dickens's Coketown was, besides being a "triumph of fact", "a town of redbrick, or of brick that would have been red if the smoke and ashes had allowed it". Soot horrified Victorian aesthetes in exactly the same way that carbon excites environmentalists today. But the Victorian cacotopia was not always defined by being dirty. To the endlessly inventive Victorian mind, novelty was often threateningly ugly. Even in the case of John Nash's coruscatingly cream Carlton House Terrace. To Owen Jones, according to Ralph Dutton's *London Homes* (1952), Nash's slightly larky and louche classicism "repeats the apparent determination of ages that there should be no external architectural beauty in London".

Ruskin's nightmarish vision was often articulated in his booming orotund Old Testament cadences, but nowhere better than *The Two Paths* (1859): "The whole of the island… set as thick with chimneys as the masts stand in the docks of Liverpool; that there shall be no meadows in it; no tree; no gardens; only a little corn grown on the house tops, reaped and threshed by the steam; that you do not even have room for roads, but travel either over the roofs of your mills, on viaducts; or under their floors, in tunnels; that, the smoke having rendered the light of the sun unserviceable, you work always by the light of your own gas; that no acre of English ground shall be without its shaft and its engine".

Opposite Carlton House Terrace, London. Owen Jones, author of *The Grammar of Ornament* (2008), said it was proof of 'the apparent determination of ages that there should be no external architectural beauty in London.'

Overleaf Stalbridge Docks, Garston, Liverpool (1906). Ruskin predicted that the whole of Great Britain would end up "set as thick with chimneys as the masts stand in the docks of Liverpool".

Long, dark passages

What precise experiences convinced Ruskin of the ugliness and the potential for ugliness in the modern world? From what experiences did he acquire his nightmarish vision of a population consigned to tunnels? Before Freud's insights, Ruskin's alarm at the prospect of long, dark passages may have gone unnoticed as an insight into his delicate sexual nature.

From about 1825 when the first shaft of Brunel's Thames Tunnel was sunk, subterranean works had in general become a symbol of progress and its problems. Mines, the close relations of tunnels in engineering terms, have been described as the womb of the Industrial Revolution, another sexual metaphor. In more and more urgent pursuit of coal, miners had to dig deeper and deeper into the Underworld, providing those sensitive to see with a dramatic symbol. Dickens's Coketown was a version of Hell: "there was a stifling smell of hot oil everywhere" and people were deafened by "the whirr of shafts and wheels".

Ruskin was only in his early 40s when the first London trial Tube ran from Edgware Road on 24 May 1862. Celebrity guests had numbers painted on their stovepipe hats. The Rt. Hon. William Ewart Gladstone was, for example, No.16. Ruskin was not on board. The world authority on Ruskin, Robert Hewison, says since Ruskin was a very rich man he probably disdained the Tube and took cabs. Certainly, there is no record of his ever having used one. He fulminated against the new railway in the Lake District and used it all the time to reach Brantwood, his house on Coniston Water. Consistency is, of course, a puerile temptation.

Battling in black floods without an ark

From the Stygian luxury of his lakeside home in a verdant north country Elysium not yet polluted by industry's smell of hot oil and infernal whirr, Ruskin could contemplate in comfort the ugliness threatening to envelop him and his less privileged countrymen. The defilement of soot and the deafening noise of cog-wheels and pistons was an all too tangible prospect of damnation. Again, it is specially interesting how the piston has so significant a place in Ruskin's demonology. Because they are contained in lubricated sleeves or cylinders (that same lubrication providing the often cited smell of hot oil which replaced sulphur as a token of the Devil's presence), Ruskin may never have actually seen a piston. But his subconscious alarm at the occult, inexhaustible sexual character of its intromittent, repetitive cycle is impossible to ignore.

The material ugliness and horror of the new cities was a recurrent theme in the nineteenth century. Driven to despair by poverty, insomnia and

Opposite London's brave new tunnels and its new underground gripped the popular imagination, offering an anteroom to Hell, as it were. Ruskin feared that one day the whole population would have to live underground. The Blackwall Tunnel, engineered by Alexander Binnie was, at 6200 feet, the world's longest underwater tunnel when it opened in 1897.

drink, in 1874 the poet James Thomson published *The City of Dreadful Night* in the *National Reformer*, a journal of materialist atheism. "O melancholy Brothers, dark, dark, dark! O battling in black floods without an ark," he writes. In his *Anthology of Invective and Abuse* (1929), Hugh Kingsmill says Thomson's despair "sprung from deeper than intellectual resources". In fact, it sprung from the aesthetic experience of the Victorian city. There they were, battling in black floods.

At this stage, technology had not yet been incorporated into cultural possibilities. So even the soot-free, piston-less telegraph seemed to threaten civilization. The Pre-Raphaelite painter Edward Burne-Jones shared Ruskin's personal distaste for many aspects of the modern world. Indeed, he believed his art was inspired by the early Renaissance. Although not a Christian, in a stylish compensatory gesture against progress's grim march, Burne-Jones said that whenever he saw a telegraph pole, he painted another angel. How charming to think that the beautiful, golden-haired angel in *Love Leading the Pilgrim* (1896–7), his last great painting, was inspired not by Bible classes, but by the sight of a creosoted larch pole.

The rhetoric of escape from urban ugliness sometimes found unusual targets. The hysteria of popular novelist Ouida (see page 94) humbles even Ruskin at his most purple. In a neglected, but richly evocative, essay entitled "The Ugliness of Modern Life" published in her *Critical Studies* (1900), Ouida joined the condemnation of Nash and modern urbanism: "It would be impossible to painters and poets to live in Regent's Park," she writes, "the Avenue de

Left The Thames Tunnel by Marc Isambard Brunel was begun in 1825 and occasionally flooded, eventually reaching completion in 1843. 50,000 people walked through it on its opening day.

Above A late-nineteenth century copy by A. Corsi Lalli of Sir Edward Coley Burne-Jones's *Love Leading the Pilgrim* (1896–7), oil on ivorine. Like Ruskin, Burne-Jones disliked the contemporary world, even with its miraculous achievements. Whenever he saw another telegraph pole, he painted another angel.

Villiers, in Cromwell Road or the Via Nazionale, or in any of the new quarters of English or continental towns, unless their instincts of beauty had become dull and dwarfed".

Amsterdam, meanwhile, is an "unmeaning mass of modern insignificance and ugliness". However, Ouida specially disliked Haussmann's Paris and the dreary monotony of the modern street. Which, of course, to another person would be a delightful symmetry and consistency. The lightwells behind Haussman's dull facades were full, she suspected (on what evidence is not clear), of ravenous parasites. The idea of living in a "flat" would be "intolerable… to anyone with a sense of the true charm of life". And she is convinced that new architecture leads to social problems: "It is natural that the people shut up in these structures crave for drink, for nameless vices, for the brothel, the opium den, the cheap eating-house and gaming-booth".

In this interpretation, beauty is natural and instinctive while ugliness is artificial and contrived. Whenever you escape from nature into modern architecture, ugliness is released. Ouida's contemporaries in her hated Paris found the Eiffel Tower ugly. In 1887 Guy de Maupassant, Charles Garnier, Charles Gounod and Alexandre Dumas, *fils*, wrote to *Le Temps* calling it a "hateful column of bolted tin… useless and monstrous". Less than 40 years before, Ruskin had condemned Joseph Paxton's magnificent hall for the Great Exhibition as an oversized greenhouse. Perhaps, even, an oversized Wardian case.

Newness, whether Nash's louche white stucco or Paxton's or Eiffel's rather different nuts and bolts, was often found ugly. Underlying this is a question the core of which is one of the central conflicts in our language and thought: the conflict, if that is what it is, of accident and design. At a London restaurant in 2009, I asked Robert A. M. Stern, Dean of the Yale School of

Architecture, if it was possible to design a deliberately ugly building. He smiled and said "Sure. It's easy. People do it all the time". But it's not in fact simple. The deliberate creation of ugliness is rare because it is so complex and demanding a task. Ask a car designer or an architect to design an ugly automobile or an ugly building and they are often stumped.

Victorian bathers knee-deep in despair

Now, complete rearrangements of our tastes have allowed us to see things differently to Ruskin or Ouida. Nash and Eiffel have long since been absorbed into genteel acceptability, even popularity. The distinction between accident and design is the same as the difference between natural and unnatural disasters. In a long-forgotten article in *Horizon* in 1946, Ernest M. Frost poetically describes the rusty Thames of the Isle of Sheppey and its sad acceptance of strange light: "Gantries and dead grass fix the sun on a skewer and the glutinous inlets of the black oily water glister with rainbows of the oily machinery standing like Victorian bathers knee-deep in despair". Is this a description of beauty or of ugliness?

Featurism and the fear of reality

Whether the product of accident or design, whether articulate or mute, a debate about what is truly ugly remains in the background of architecture and design rhetoric. Australia's greatest architectural critic, Robin Boyd, was even bold enough to make a talking point of his country's ugliness, although he was not the first to do so. Anthony Trollope said: "It is taken for granted that Australia is ugly". In *The Australian Ugliness* (1960), Boyd, author of a monograph on Kenzo Tange, coins the expression "featurism". This is the enemy of understatement and plainness. It is a sort of superficial beautifying… And superficial beautifying is very difficult to distinguish from profound uglification.

"The visual arts", Boyd says, "cannot rid the world of evil and ugliness, and they should not be interested in applying pleasing cosmetics to the face of a sick patient. They are doing well if they can portray, honestly, richly and vividly the world as it is… the Australian ugliness begins with fear of reality". So here is a link to the Victorian unease with the contemporary world. And Boyd also makes the significant point: "as nature gets visually lovelier, man's habits grow visually viler".

Anyone who has made even a casual study of the vernacular architecture of coastal Cornwall or Wales would agree.

26585 BETWS · Y · COED, UGLY HOUSE.

THE UGLY HOUSE

JUDGES LTD

Above *The Hypnerotomachia Polifili* (1499), a romance said to be by Francesco Colonna. This illustrated Renaissance curiosity may be the cultural source for our affection for ruins.

Previous An ugly house in Betws-y-Coed, Wales. There is no consistent relationship between magnificent landscape and artificial beauty. Indeed, any inspection of Snowdonia's vernacular architecture suggests quite the opposite: the human response to awesome Nature is often crabbed and defiant.

We now enjoy a sort of weird approval for ruination. The beauty of ruins themselves has often been noted: according to Kenneth Clark, the first painting of a ruin was Maso di Bianco's St Sylvester and the Dragon of 1340 in Santa Croce, Florence. A little later in the Renaissance, the famous *Hypnerotomachia Poliphili* of 1467 treated ruins elegiacally and is often cited as the source for "Ruins, beauty of", becoming a fixed idea in the Romantic conception of the world, or, at least in the indexes of books that describe it. The taste for ruins continues, but has shapeshifted somewhat. In his classic of collector's monomania, *Boring Postcards* (1999), Martin Parr, a photographer who romanticizes distress, displays a genius for man-made ugliness. He reproduces the interchange of I-75, I-85 and I-20 in Atlanta. A bridge over the Pennsylvania Turnpike is in frank contradiction with the nostrums of functionalist theory which claim that engineering is inevitably beautiful. Well, as Parr shows, sometimes it is not.

One postcard is even titled "Traveling on Beautiful Interstate 35". No life, not even traffic, is on show. The blue sky has puffy clouds and the photographer has planted his tripod on the centre line in the middle of the highway to achieve an effect of perfectly symmetrical and stultifying banality. A clunking concrete bridge lies heavily across the road. The grass is green, but looks artificial. Strange, really how it is possible to write even as much as this about so very little.

The miracle of the superhighways such as I-75, according to P. J. O'Rourke, was that there was no view. As Alice B. Toklas says, at least according to Gertrude Stein, "I like a view but I like to sit with my back turned to it". O'Rourke says natural beauty is boring. Scenery? Pah! "You look at a beautiful vista and, all right, it's beautiful. Now what? After 30 seconds you begin to fidget. You wish you had a book, a Sony Walkman, even a Taco Bell double dogfood enchilada". Besides, the other problem with nature's bounty as seen from the Interstate is that "Swivel your head to capture the beauty and you'll hit a bridge abutment".

tiful Interstate 35

Freedom to make everything look like shit

Or take the Winrock Shopping Center in Albuquerque, New Mexico, another postcard in Parr's collection. It looks military, but not in a good way. Or "The Colourful Rug near the entrance of the national offices of the American Baptist churches, Valley Forge Interchange, PA". This is specially moving placed opposite "The beautiful and spacious dining room of the Wesleyan Retirement Home in Georgetown, Texas". What aesthetic is at work here? Or Bentonville, Arkansas, before and after WalMart: the injection of great wealth did not in any way reduce the intense banality of the townscape. How can such stupefying tedium simultaneously be so compelling? Mind, you could say the same of the horror of car crashes, which fascinate even as they repel.

One answer comes from P. J. O'Rourke in *Driving Like Crazy* (2009): "This is America, and that's freedom for you – freedom to make everything look like shit, perhaps, but freedom nonetheless. Are we going to bulldoze every Kmart and create a federal agency to design something in its place? That was how East Berlin became the charming place it was. Dairy Queens, water slides, flea markets, Cinema 1-2-3-4-5-6s – they are our family. They may be ugly and embarrassing but we wouldn't be here without them. Americans just love this stuff".

Thus, the Zen of crap. But would Far Horizons Trailer Village in Tucson or the Celanese plant between Kingsville and Bishop, Texas, be relieved of their ugly horror if nature overwhelmed them, if their concrete paths and pipe manifolds and distillation towers fell into desuetude and creepers covered the rusting metal and faded vinyl and other crap?

These natural softenings or improvements were the classic effects of ruin that Rose Macaulay described as "enjungled" in her fetishized account, *Pleasure of Ruins* (1953). She writes pleasurably about exploring a ruin and finding a bestiary of dragons, satyrs, screech-owls, serpents, speckled toads and foxes. Today in a modern ruin, such as a landfill, we might find not Macaulay's trees thrusting through the empty window sockets, the rose-bay and fennel blossoming within the broken walls, the brambles tangling outside. We will more likely find a stained microwave, some old tyres, plastic bottles and crisp packets.

The problem with new ruins is that they have not acquired a patina of respectable age and are only slowly being softened by art. John Piper recorded the blitzed Coventry Cathedral, ruined by the Luftwaffe in 1940, but it was a sentimental vision. The contemporary taste for urban crap is more confrontational.

The artist Robert Smithson was an exponent of "anti-aesthetics" or "pro-ugliness". In pursuit of ugliness, he was interested in natural deformities, nature's own devaluation of its store of beauty. The best sites

Below The Dairy Queen soft serve franchise was launched in Joliet, Illinois, 1940. There are now nearly 6000 stores worldwide and the largest is in Riyadh, Saudi Arabia.

Opposite and above Postcard of Coventry showing the postwar rebuild of the city (c.1960), and the new Cathedral today: new ruins have not acquired the agreeable patina of art. The devastated medieval Coventry Cathedral was replaced by Basil Spence's masterpiece, although it was not to everyone's taste: the critic Reyner Banham called it a "ring-a-ding God-box".

for the "earth art" he expounded are ones ruined by rapacious industrialization and its after-effects. This is what a poet noticed on the Isle of Sheppey 60 years ago. Lara Almarcegui has published books on modern ruins including *Wastelands Map Amsterdam: Guide to the Empty Sites of Amsterdam* (1999) and *Ruins in the Netherlands* (2005). She wants industrial ruins in Genk and Rotterdam to remain rubbish. She despairs that fascinating wastelands are sometimes developed and "improved".

Is beauty boring? And is ugliness exciting? Edmund Burke's interest in pain and fear brought two aspects of ugliness into the realm of aesthetics. Tunnels, soot, pistons, rubbish and ruins continue the job he began in his study *On the Sublime and Beautiful* (1756).

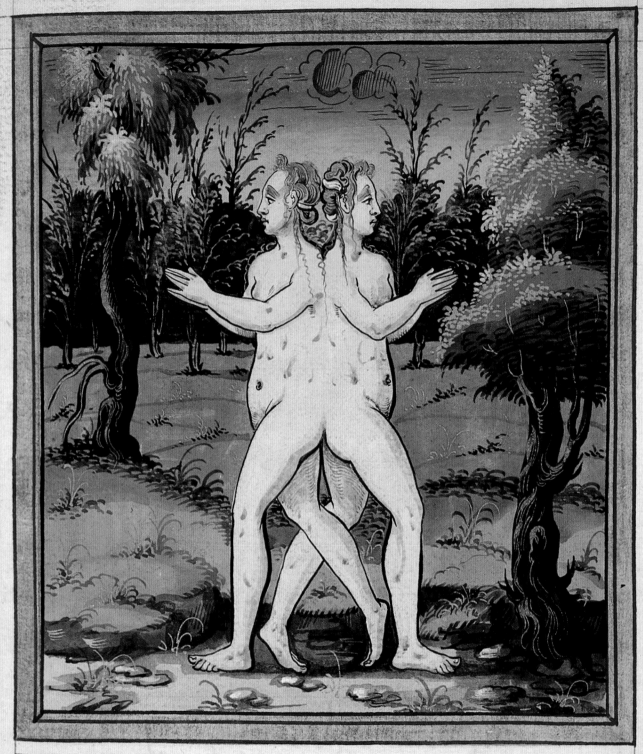

ES INDIENS & Brachmanes ancien-
nement se sont monstres fort ceremonieux en
lobseruation des natiuitez de leurs enfans. Car

8.

What's Wrong with Beauty, or Unnatural Selection

Opposite Conjoined twins from
Pierre Boaistuau's *Histoires
Prodigieuses* (1560) an example
of the popular 'wonder book.'
Boaistuau says "There is nothing
to be seen which more stirreth
the spirit of man... than monsters,
wonders and abominations".
Accidents of nature ask the
question if ugliness is itself an
accident, and the obverse: is
beauty always designed?

Why is racism ugly?
Is beauty a career advantage?
Should ugliness be eradicated?

It is important to separate the idea of the freak, or accident of nature, from the rather different matter of ugliness. Freaks are the product of genetic calamities. Ugliness is more complicated since it has a social and cultural rather than merely medical character.

The reason? Ugliness is rarely accidental. Fundamental to the idea of the ugly are notions of deliberation, intention and purpose. It is a very sophisticated idea, inaccessible perhaps to Fred Flintstone, since to consider something ugly you must be aware of the alternatives. To call something ugly suggests you have an established range of preferences. Physical deformation, for example, may be unpleasant, even distressing, but lacks the deliberate expressive intention of ugliness. This, as ever, returns us to the etymology of the word "ugly" in the Norse *ugga*, meaning aggressive.

But accidents of nature and aggression-by-design have often been confused. The European mind has long been fascinated by freaks: Pierre Boaistuau's *Histoires Prodigieuses* (1560) is only one of the most well known, with its famous woodcuts of conjoined twins and other unfortunates – a sort of late-medieval freak show.

The problem with hair

Disorders which now have a scientific name – hypertrichosis, or excessive hair growth, for example – were once construed not as an ailment which might be beneficially treated with hormones, but as an expression of something more sinister. Hypertrichosis was the medical origin of the ape woman phenomenon which, with fascinated revulsion, preoccupied a part of the European imagination until shaving, plucking, epilation, depilation, electrolysis and laser removal replaced medieval fear.

Still, abnormal hair retains a disturbing power. The monster in *I Was a Teenage Werewolf* (1957) would not be so scary if it were less hairy. And Pat Suzuki's curious character – inspired by Vercors's *Les Animaux Dénaturés* – in *Skullduggery* (1970), has weird, feral eroticism because hirsutism is, incongruously, matched with nudity.

An excess of hair in the wrong places has always been a matter of revulsion, but other characteristics – not quite deformities, but distinguishing features – have also been exploited in political propaganda. Stooping gaits, greasy beards, exaggerated features and sallow skin might be examples. Indeed, in 1930 the NSDAP decided that film might advance its racial theories, and went on to politicize ugliness through propaganda.

Opposite The horror film *I Was a Teenage Werewolf* (press photo, 1957) was a double release with *Invasion of the Saucer Men* (1957). It plays on popular anxieties about regression to a pre-technical past and relies on hair to provide some of its anxious semantics.

Overleaf Hypertrichosis is abnormally excessive hair growth. The original "Bearded Woman" was Annie Jones, who belonged to Barnum & Bailey Circus and acted as spokeswoman for its freaks.

PUB-9
#201-178

JEW SÜSS

(From the Novel by LEON FEUCHTWANGER)

WITH

CONRAD VEIDT
FRANK VOSPER
CEDRIC HARDWICKE
BENITA HUME
GERALD DU MAURIER
PAMELA OSTRER
JOAN MAUDE
MARY CLARE
EVA MOORE
FRANK CELLIER
SAM LIVESAY
HELENA PICKARD
GIBB McLAUGHLIN
PAUL GRAETZ
ROBERT NAINBY
HELEN FERRERS
HENRY HALLETT
RANDLE AYRTON

Directed by LOTHAR MENDES

A Gaumont-British Picture

CONRAD VEIDT and GIBB McLAUGHLIN in "JEW SÜSS"

Above Programme for the original 1934 film *Jew Süss* by British director Lothar Mendes, which condemned anti-Semitic behaviour, unlike Goebbels's notorious anti-Semitic version of 1940, which used "racially pure" Jewish extras rounded-up from the Prague ghetto and coerced into starring. But even the 1934 version did not openly criticize the persecution of the Jews as strongly as the original novel: censors were afraid that too vocal a condemnation of the German government's policies would result in diplomatic trouble.

Opposite Still from Leni Riefenstahl's *Olympia* (1936), a documentary on the Berlin Olympics. This javelin-thrower represented an idealized version of "Aryan" beauty. Muscular, naked blondes strutting in Valhalla were active in the imaginations of the leading Nazi thinkers.

Joseph Goebbels, Reichsminister for Propaganda, had three pet (if that is the right word) anti-semitic film projects. One was *Die Rothschilds* (1940), but more infamous were *Jew Süss* (1940) and *Der ewige Jude* (1940). These were construed as negative counterparts to Leni Riefenstahl's two great propaganda hits, *Triumph des Willens* (1935), her choreographed account of the 1934 Nazi rally at Nuremburg, and *Olympia: Fest der Völker* (1936), her stylized and even more choreographed documentary of the 1936 Berlin Olympics. The Riefenstahl films presented an ideal of "Aryan" beauty: muscular blondes strut in Valhalla; Teutonic maidens synchronize their biceps. The Jewish films, by contrast, presented cartoonish stereotypes of the hairy, furrowed, drooling, sleazy, grasping, hook-nosed, semite-rapists. They were, quite literally, required viewing for the SS.

The *Jew Süss* story is an interesting miniature in the story of prejudice and its interpretations. Joseph Süss Oppenheimer was a real eighteenth century financier of a buccaneering style who, having inadvertently betrayed a young Jewish girl, nobly accepts his sentence to the gallows – even as he discovers he is not Jewish himself. Lion Feuchtwanger, a Jew, wrote a novel on Süss in 1925. Paul Kornfeld turned the story into a play in 1930 and *Jew*

ENTARTETE "KUNST"

Ausstellungsführer

PREIS 30 PFG.

Opposite Ideas of "degeneration" animated Nazi thought. Culturally speaking, this culminated in the *Entartete Kunst* (Degenerate Art) exhibition, which opened in Munich in 1937. It made a mockery of jazz, abstraction and atonal music as well as of its Jewish, Bolshevik and black instigators.

Overleaf left E. McKnight Kauffer's anti-German propaganda for the US Office of Inter-American Affairs (c.1944). The copyline is "The New Order of the Axis". The Nazi is drooling, as they so often do in propaganda.

Overleaf right Arthur Szyk's anti-Japanese propaganda on the cover of *Collier's* magazine (December 1942). The cartoonish Japanese officer has fangs and wings like a bat.

Süss became a movie by British director Lothar Mendes in 1934.

All these treatments were sympathetic to the subtleties of Jewish identity, thus appalled Goebbels who set out with maximum commitment, if not distinction, to make the most "successful" anti-Semitic film of all time. "Racially pure" Jews were rounded up from the Prague ghetto for the 1940 production (which won a Golden Lion at the Venice Film Festival of that year). It was Goebbels's intention to caricature the Jews so as to persuade the *Volk* that, as he helpfully explained in a 1942 speech: "every Jew is our enemy… regardless of whether he vegetates in a Polish ghetto or carries on his parasitic existence in Berlin… or blows the trumpets of war in New York".

Jud Süss was followed by another Goebbels propaganda hit, *Der ewige Jude* (The Eternal Jew) in 1940. Here, thoughtfully expanding his visual vocabulary of degradation, Goebbels instructed his film-makers to show Jews lurking furtively in cellars as humanoid rats. Meanwhile, the Nazis had edited the history of art to support their views on beauty and ugliness. In 1937 at the Haus der Kunst in Munich a notorious exhibition called *Entartete Kunst* (Degenerate Art) opened.

Degeneration had been a preoccupation of Nazi thought since the publication in 1892 of Max Nordau's *Entartung* (Degeneration), a farrago of pseudo-scientific semi-mystical pottiness. Although he was himself Jewish (indeed, the conceptor of "The Muscle Jew", a type he advanced on the world in a 1900 article in the *Jewish Gymnastic Journal*), Nordau's brooding speculations on the psycopathology of late nineteenth century art helped legitimize Nazi theories.

In the Degenerate Art exhibition, works by Africans and Jews, together with degenerate Nordics, including the Expressionist Emil Nolde, were lampooned. Sculptures by Jacob Epstein, who specialized in robust primitivist nudes, were specially selected for vilification. In the sometimes confused contest between ugliness and beauty, the contrast between Epstein's muscular grunt and the queasy classicism of Nazi-favourite sculptor Arno Breker presents a moment, *circa* 1937, of relevant clarity.

For once being honest, Hitler declared that propaganda need, by way of contrast, never be "honest". Unsurprisingly, the Allies were also guilty of lies and distortion in pursuit of military and political objectives. In the heat of the Second World War, what with its pistons and stink of hot oil, it was necessary to uglify the enemy as if the essential message of the Blitz or Pearl Harbor had been forgotten by the public. Stereotyping the enemy as ugly was perhaps even more motivating than having the enemy drop bombs on you.

For example, the Office of Inter-American Affairs commissioned posters from the distinguished graphic designer E. McKnight Kauffer in 1944. *The New Order of the Axis* shows a pointy-headed, bespectacled, dribbling profile of a chinless German whose aesthetic particulars plumb goodness knows what depths of the contemporary psyche. At about the same time,

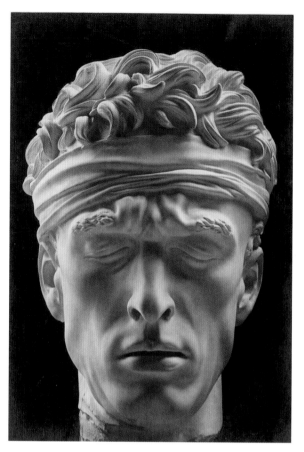

a Decca record was entitled "We're Gonna Have to Slap the Dirty Little Jap". A 1942 edition of *Collier's* has a very nasty American stereotype of the Japanese on the cover. Slit eyes, sharp teeth and drooling were commonplace in the uglification of enemies.

Why bother to be beautiful?

Propaganda exploited the relationship that exists in the primitive mind between conventional notions of ugliness and conventional notions of badness. Yet troublesome as it is to establish working definitions of either beauty or ugliness, there are answers to the question "why bother to be beautiful" outside the scope of evolutionary biology. The economists Markus M. Mobius and Tanya S. Rosenblat published an article in *The American Economic Review* in 2006 called "Why Beauty Matters". They say there is, in the world of employment, a "beauty premium". An experiment was set up where workers were required to solve a problem about mazes, one which required only intelligence and application. However, it soon became clear that employers preferred beautiful people, irrespective of their problem-solving ability.

Mobius and Rosenblat say the beauty premium works three ways:

1. Beautiful workers are more confident and this has a self-fulfilling effect: higher confidence makes a beautiful worker doubly attractive.

2. For a given level of skill, the beautiful worker is more highly regarded.

3. At a similar level of confidence, beautiful workers have interpersonal skills in conversation and manners that often lead to higher pay – often 10 per cent more.

Anthony Synnott, a sociologist at Montreal's Concordia University, studies our prejudices about beauty and ugliness. He says that ugly people are presumed to be less sensitive, interesting, exciting and sexual than beautiful ones. The prejudice may have cultural origins in fairy tales where wicked characters are inevitably made grotesque, deformed. Some related research has shown that parental insistence on seatbelt use is proportional to the ugliness of the child. Beauty gets belted up.

Ugly like us

Beauty as a remedy for ugliness is an idea which now has a technological as well as a metaphysical character. When Catherine Denueve said, 'After 40, it's your arse or your face,' the actress was referring to the depredations age makes on physique and physiognomy. She might also have been hinting where, if on a budget, you might like to prioritize the interventions of liposuction or full-facial laser resurfacing.

In 2008 a successful Connecticut cosmetic surgeon called Laurence Kirwan (full declaration: a school and university friend of mine) caused international outrage when, in a feature in the *Mail on Sunday*, he was suggested to have considered operating on his Down's Syndrome daughter, Ophelia, so she could become "beautiful like us".

The writer of the article was Bonnie Estridge (and an article of similar substance was published in 2006 by *Grazia*, later publishing a corrective letter). Replying over the internet, Dr Kirwan said he had been traduced: "They have taken what was described as a thoughtful Mother's Day piece about a mother and her disabled daughter (who is about to face surgery for enlarged tonsils) and converted it by means of innuendo and lies into a controversy about cosmetic surgery on children with Down's Syndrome. Both I and Chelsea [Ophelia's mother] agreed to participate in this article only on the understanding that it would promote research into Down's Syndrome".

Dr Kirwan called the manipulation of his interview sensationalist, tasteless and insensitive. He never uttered the words that became the article's title "Should we use Plastic Surgery to Make Our Down's Daughter Beautiful

Like Us?" At the time, Dr Kirwan was considering giving another daughter a nose job. Of Ophelia he says, "Chelsea and I love Ophelia as she is, not as we would hope her to become". Plastic surgery for children with congenital deformities – cleft lip, for example – is well established, and Dr Kirwan has a distinguished record of charitable work in restorative surgery.

He writes, balancing technical imperatives with relativism: "As an admirer of art and aesthetics I find beauty in every individual. As a physician, I have spent a great deal of my life helping individuals improve the quality of their life…In addition, a child is and should always be beautiful to its parents".

Surgical procedures on adult Down's Syndrome patients are already familiar, but perhaps a little less controversial than those on children. But aesthetic interventions at any stage in life invite the inevitable and unsettling prospect of cosmetic abortions. A weird mirror image of this quest for surgically enhanced – or even surgically created – beauty is the matter of people who volunteer for ugliness: what you might call elective uglification. To adapt the concept attributed to Dr Kirwan, do you want to be ugly like us? Popular culture suggests that many people do.

Nipples the shape of Soviet stars

When Punk solidified, if that is the right word, in 1976, it was remarkable evidence of the will to ugliness. In *Lipstick Traces* Greil Marcus says, 'It's hard to remember how ugly the first punks were.' He goes on to describe a culturally condoned interest in body perforations, vomiting, pockmarks, acne, bad posture, stuttering, disability and, of course, tattoos.

The enormous scope for uglification via the tattoo was illustrated in Danzig Baldaev and Sergey Vasiliev's magnificent *Russian Criminal Tattoo Encyclopedia* (2003). A thief's tattooed body, they say, is the equivalent of military regalia. A sort of service record from corrective labour colonies and cell blocks. One example shows, as a purely arbitrary example, the upper half of a woman. Bare-breasted, she has nipples the shape of Soviet stars, pig's ears and features, with a hammer and sickle on her forehead: a tattoo within a tattoo. She is encircled by barbed wire and the legend "A Russian woman convict is a red Soviet swine who doesn't like work and thinks she is a higher race; she is malicious and envious, abandons her own children, loves getting drunk, thieving, acting like a hooligan and humiliating everyone". Meanwhile, even as the FDA reports that 45 million Americans have uglified themselves with tattoos, Americans were suffering tattoo remorse. One estimate is 100,000 laser removal treatments annually.

In the modern mind, the will to decorate – whether human bodies, or buildings or machines – became mixed up with the will to defile them.

Opposite Drawing from the *Russian Criminal Tattoo Encyclopedia Volume I* (2003) by FUEL and Danzig Baldaev. Jailhouse tatts advertise tribal loyalties and are an aid to self-expression for the inarticulate. The relationship between criminality and a taste for the tattoo is suggested by the extraordinarily vigorous tradition of body art within the Russian penitential system.

Overleaf London's punk movement of the 1970s celebrated swearing, spitting, confrontation and generally refused any form of elegance. Malcolm McLaren, the punk impresario, said of one of his clients: 'They are so bad they are good.'

From the idea that machine-made decoration, since it was, according to Pazaurek's Principles a "fake", was in some sense immoral, a connection was soon made to ugliness. This is an area where human vanity and design principles collide: cosmetic abortions vying for attention with an architecture based on the fantasy of functionalism.

Be that as it may, this business of worrying about ugliness is a defining characteristic of the contemporary mind. The medieval mind was taught to equate beauty with divinity; but the core belief of the Modernists that ugliness could be avoided if only architects and designers could concentrate on the absolute, structural essence of buildings and products has an almost religious character. Beauty lies in fundamentals while ugliness, as it were, was only skin-deep.

Ornament is crime (the ugly couple)

That this became a near religious belief is suggested in the title of Art Nouveau architect Henri van de Velde's *Kunstgewerbliche Laienpredigten* (1902), which translates very simply as "Arty Lay Sermons". Here Van de Velde elaborates on his ideas in fantastical, cod Biblical language. This is one of the key texts essential to an understanding of early twentieth century ideas on the theory and practice of uglification. Preachily, Van de Velde writes: "Thou shalt comprehend the form and construction of all objects only in the sense of their strictest, elementary logic and justification for their existence… and if thou art animated by the wish to beautify these forms… give thyself to the longing for refinement to which thy aesthetic sensibility or taste for ornament… shall inspire thee, only so far as thou canst respect and retain the rights and the essential appearance of these forms and constructions!"

Deadening inheritance

This polemic was developed the following year in the most extreme expression yet of the idea that decoration was bad for you and your house. This was the Austrian architect Adolf Loos's 1908 essay "Ornament und Verbrechen" (Ornament and Crime). Perhaps not much read in its day, certainly not much read now, but in the most influential histories of architecture and design, by Reyner Banham and Kenneth Frampton, for example, Loos is given a role that has impressed students ever since. Adolf Loos had spent three years in the United States and been impressed by the pistonnage of an architectural culture free of the deadening inheritance of temples and cathedrals. He was very taken by Louis Sullivan's remark, "It could only benefit us if for a time we were to abandon ornament and concentrate entirely on the

Opposite Adolf Loos's "Ornament and Crime" (1908) (pictured is a poster for a 1913 lecture) mingled design theory with criminal investigation. It was typical of the Viennese culture that produced Freud. Loos found a synergy between middle-class taste, very much based upon English exemplars, and his idea of aesthetic perfection. At the same time, medical researchers were studying the physiognomy of recidivists.

VORTRAG
VERANSTALTET VOM AKAD. ARCHITEKTEN VEREIN.
ADOLF LOOS:
ORNAMENT UND VERBRECHEN.
FREITAG, DEN 21. FEBRUAR 1913, ½8h ABENDS IM FESTSAAL DES ÖSTERR. ING. U. ARCH. VEREINES, I. ESCHENBACHGASSE 9. KARTEN ZU 5, 4, 3, 2, 1 K BEI KEHLENDÖRFER
12. MÄRZ: MISS LEVETUS: ALTENGL. KATHEDRALEN.
MITTE MÄRZ: DR. HABERFELD: ÜBER ADOLF LOOS.

erection of buildings that were finely shaped and charming in their sobriety".

So here is another connection between "clean lines" (not to mention clean bodies) and moral superiority: the metaphor of drunkenness in Van de Velde's last sentence is surely revealing. Beauty has a purity in behavior as well as appearance. In "Ornament and Crime", a slightly potty rant, Loos is particularly exercised by voluntary human uglification: "The child is amoral. To our eyes, the Papuan is too. The Papuan kills his enemies and eats them. He is not a criminal. But when modern man kills someone and eats him he is either a criminal or a degenerate. The Papuan tattoos his skin, his boat, his paddles, in short everything he can lay his hands on. He is not a criminal. The modern man who tattoos himself is either a criminal or a degenerate. There are prisons in which 80 per cent of the inmates show tattoos. The tattooed who are not in prison are latent criminals or degenerate aristocrats. If someone who is tattooed dies at liberty, it means he has died a few years before committing a murder".

Hypertrichosis, uglification, Down's Syndrome and tattoos are certainly a challenge to elite models of beauty, but all have their explanation in Darwin's theory. Most rudely put, evolutionary biology argues that we avoid hairy individuals or those we suspect of latent or actual criminality, or others possessing physical or intellectual flaws which we find uncongenial, because they will not make good mates. We want to breed from top quality stock.

This was the basis for the best explanation of beauty. And so it is, at the same time the best explanation of ugliness. The source is the literary critic Elaine Scarry who says, "Beauty brings copies of itself into being". We know something is beautiful if we want more of it, whether it is an attractive person or a desirable object. Professor Scarry's observation is acute, but Shakespeare did get there first. In Sonnet I he writes:

"From fairest creatures we desire increase
That therefore beauty's rose may never die".

When it comes to beauty, more is more. Even if it is a bore.

9.

Form Follows Feeling, or The Tropes Don't Work

Is Modernism a cure for ugliness?
Or is it just a matter of taste?
Is it better to be interesting or good?

Alice was having a conversation with the Gryphon and the Mock Turtle
in one of her adventures in Wonderland. The Gryphon says to her: "Never
heard of uglifying! You know what to beautify is, I suppose?'"
Alice replies: "Yes, it means to make something prettier". So the Gryphon goes:
"Well, then, if you don't know what uglify is, you are a simpleton".

Why do so many people – not all simpletons – find modern art and
architecture so aggressively ugly?

Modernism was meant to be a cure for the ills of industrial uglification,
a mounting crescendo of soot, pistons and noise reaching its peak as Lewis
Carroll was creating *Alice's Adventures in Wonderland* in the spired comfort of
Oxford. (To be realistic: the very day after the mysterious *Wonderland* was
published in 1865, the UK passed the world's first and very matter-of-fact law
about the maximum speed of vehicles.) At about the same time as *Wonderland*,
art began to look for ugliness too.

Throughout the later nineteenth century, a search for "truth" began to
preoccupy artists of advanced tastes. Truth might necessarily be ugly rather
than beautiful. This inevitably led to the exploration of neurotic states just then
becoming the province of investigative science.

The cranky pseudo-science of early alienists and pre-Freudian psychologists
provides a stimulating context to consider the evolving philosophies of
Modernism. Max Nordau, a disciple of Cesare Lombroso, the pioneer
of physiognomy as a key to character, and a contributor to Hitler's racially
biased art theory, knew exactly what the problem was. He writes: "The feeble,
the degenerate will perish; the strong will adapt themselves to the acquisition of
civilizations… The aberrations of art have no future. They will disappear when
civilized humanity shall have triumphed over its exhausted condition. The art
of the twentieth century will connect at every point with the past".

Opposite Max Nordau, author
of *Entartung* (1908). Nordau's
brooding speculations on the
psychopathology of late nineteenth
century art fed directly into Nazi
theory.

The suppurations of parasites

In his book *Degeneration*, Nordau castigates the spirit of the *fin de siècle*
without realizing that his own mannered, purple prose and operatic posturing
are, themselves, symptoms of the decadent disease he seeks to cure. The
problem, he continues, is one of 'false realism'. This is characterized by
'pessimism and the irresistible tendency to licentious ideas, and the most
vulgar and unclean modes of expression'. He compares, colourfully, the
afflictions of late nineteenth century culture to the afflictions of a body
suffering the mortal suppurations of parasites – rather as the presence of

streptococcus and staphylococcus render a body vulnerable to influenza. At about the same time, but with more positive results, Giacomo Puccini was also saying art is disease, and the Trieste novelist Italo Svevo found himself fascinated by the pathology of Basedow's disease. In Anglophone territories this is more usually known as Graves' disease, the name of the type of hyperthyroidism that leads to accelerated bone remodelling and occasionally grotesque distortions.

Meanwhile, Munch painted anxiety; Seurat dabbled with neurology. Rather later, Picasso played with fragmentation and perceptions as atomic theory became apparent, and the Surrealists travelled into the disturbing world of dreams while holding hands with Sigmund Freud. Architects and designers, at the same time, began to explore the essence of structure which was their version of "truth". And here was a truth to replace the natural world that had been subjugated by industry and urbanization. Architects and designers were, on the whole, more optimistic than painters. And more committed to the pursuit of beauty and the eradication of ugliness, not to mention morbid states, pessimism, licentious ideas, vulgar modes of expression and the suppurations of parasites.

This was the moment when architecture and design usurped painting's traditional role as a channel for ideas about the beautiful. Modernism in architecture and design was meant to be a return to order after the chaos and muddle of the nineteenth century's promiscuity with styles and its preference for shiny brown furniture. Modernist buildings were, according to Le Corbusier, meant to be evidence of "the learned game, correct and magnificent, of form assembled in light".

That's a compelling definition and few sensible people would deny allegiance to it. Certainly, Palladio and Wren would have no argument with it. And anyone who has visited Notre-Dame-du-Haut near Besançon, or the monastery of La Tourette at Eveux-sur-Arbresle can see magic at work. At once, Le Corbusier took inspiration from the clean lines and rational shapes of aircraft, but was inspired also by the magnificent Cistercian foundations at Le Thoronet, Sénanque and Silvacane in the serene wooded hills of the Var.

My debate with the Mock Turtle

These monasteries are abstractions of perfect geometry, of forms assembled in light, of building as a demonstration of very elevated purpose and it is unimaginable that anyone, even a Mock Turtle, might find them less than exalting. Certainly, that was how Le Corbusier construed them. But somehow Le Corbusier and his followers became identified as apostles of ugliness, betrayers of tradition and extreme uglifiers. When the French *banlieues* erupted in civil unrest in the early twenty-first century, the flashpoint was a housing estate at Toulouse-le-Mirail, a project by disciples of Le Corbusier. True, the grim begrimed overhead concrete walkways and threatening towers make a poor comparison with Le Thoronet's divine cloisters.

The question of the world becoming uglier (by design) has its origins at the moment when consumer choice, or a version of it, first became a human possibility. When the vast new furniture stores opened in the cities, it was the beginning of the historical era when people, as the slur goes, began to buy their own furniture (instead of more nobly inheriting it). There were those Paris arcades where Zola's Nana had her nose up against the glass, ogling the fancy goods… just as her customers had ogled her.

The crossover between human prostitution and the prostitution of goods is significant. Prostitution may be the oldest profession, but it was bureaucratically systematized in France at just the same moment when the department stores were systematizing merchandise and the museums were systematizing plants, shells and animal skeletons.

With consumer choice in architecture and design came consumer doubt in these same matters, although it took a while to evolve. Before the mid-nineteenth century, hostile criticism of architecture and design was unusual. It was quite possible at one moment in history that a new building would not be noticed any more than, say, a new tree. They did not have conservationists or critics in the eighteenth century. These modern phenomena of human resources are self-appointed agents in the battle against ugliness.

Then there was a schism. The modern world comprised. As Hans Sedlmayr explained in *The Death of Light* (1964), there emerged "a characteristically provocative ugliness… during no past era did man consider the expressive forms of architecture with disgust and aversion… until the classical period, building was a natural function". The implication is clear. When things cease to be natural, they become ugly!

Johann Karl Friedrich Rosenkranz was a follower of the philosopher Hegel and, dedicated to the study of his mentor's baffling methods, had the chair of philosophy at the University of Königsberg from 1833. Among numerous unfathomable philosophical inquiries, his *Ästhetik des Hässlichen* (1853) was among the very first books to tackle the question of ugliness.

The chamber pot of horrors

In Britain, the domestic interior – not the philosophical seminar – was the battleground between beauty and ugliness. Deborah Cohen coined the term "middle-class self-fashioning" in her book *Household Gods: The British and their Possessions* (2006). In *Household Words*, the weekly journal Charles Dickens edited between 1850 and 1859, Dickens often ruminated on, say, the

Above The many faces of concrete. Toulouse-Le-Mirail (constructed 1968), designed by students of Le Corbusier. Exaltation on the one hand (see Le Corbusier's chapel, previous page), crushing tedium on the other. Toulouse-le-Mirail was a flashpoint for the Chirac-era riots in 2005, when a state of emergency was declared in parts of France.

MEN OF THE DAY, No. 29.

"King Cole."

interior of a cottage in Brixton and what it said of its occupants' tastes. *Household Words* was, incidentally, intended to act as an improving tool for the unlettered working classes, but in the event turned out to be almost exclusively middle-class in its scope, range and purpose. In his novel *Great Expectations* (1861), Dickens contrasts Wemmick's twee Gothic cottage in Walworth with the Jaggers' more austere Soho house and a moral point has been made. It was agreed among the literate and educated classes that better homes make better people. And it was in this context of improvement that Henry Cole and Richard Redgrave created their Chamber of Horrors at the Museum of Ornamental Art (the Victoria and Albert Museum) in London. Based on the surplus from the Great Exhibition at Crystal Palace (Ruskin's oversized greenhouse), the Chamber of Horrors put on display objects designed on "false principles". It opened in 1852 and, committed to instructing both consumers and manufacturers on "the correct principles of taste", it was a wholly original warning.

It was the moment when design-as-an-improving force became institutionalized – although "false principles" were not always completely eradicated. Henry Cole's other memento of the Great Exhibition was the Albert Memorial, built on its site in Kensington Gardens. Unpopular by the time it opened in 1876, it is now one of the great attractions of London. The Albert Memorial, it turns out, was a monument not just to a princely ideal, but to an altogether larger idea: the one thing certain about taste is that it changes.

Be that as it may, soon after his death in 1882 Cole was credited with what Elizabeth Bonython called "miraculous powers as a reformer in taste". Because of his efforts at the Department of Science and Art, a writer of 1885 claimed, "The English people were converted from Philistinism, and became ardent lovers of art. In the poorest cottages may now be found vessels of artistic design and other delights of the eye, as cheap as the ugly patterns obtained everywhere except in the houses of the richest a few years ago".

This may well have overstated the revolution in the domestic style of his countrymen, but Cole's determination to eradicate ugliness in consumer affairs was certainly influential in Europe. In 1909 Gustav E. Pazaurek, director of Stuttgart's State Crafts Museum, opened what is variously translated as his "Museum of Art Indiscretions" or his "Cabinet of Bad Taste". Writing in the journal *Der Kunstwart* in 1899, Pazaurek, also a dramatist and poet, explained that every museum should have a torture chamber, a chamber of horrors, to educate those with a thick aesthetic skin. Accordingly, Pazaurek collected over 900 ugly objects. In 1933, over the objections of its creator, the collection was withdrawn and put into storage.

For the centenary, the Museum der Dinge in Berlin made the first attempt to reconstruct the original from the 700 or so surviving objects, inviting visiting Berliners to contribute examples of contemporary design atrocities or

examples of industrialized ugliness. With magnificent German thoroughness, Pazaurek had established a systematic checklist to describe aesthetic crimes. Although his views were inevitably formed by very different circumstances (in the Germany of 1909 the proto-Modernism of the Deutscher Werkbund was tussling, not always successfully, with a democratic preference for Jodelstil), officials at the Museum der Dinge found that the 1909 checklist remains curiously relevant as a test for taste.

Pazaurek's Prinzip

Pazaurek determined that there were five categories of errors that could lead to ugliness: Material Mistakes, Design Mistakes, Decorative Mistakes, Kitsch Mistakes and Contemporary Mistakes. The list is too German to reproduce in full, but an edited version – presented almost in poetic form – nonetheless reveals some of the persuasive force of his reasoning.

Material mistakes
- Inferior materials, knotty wood, poor alloys, toxic substances, cheap processes, concealed flaws, distorted moulds, spotted glaze.
- Objects made of human or animal parts including bone, skin, fingernails, rhino horns, ostrich eggs, antlers, teeth, vertebrae, feathers, fish scales, lizards, lobster claws, butterflies and beetles, egg membrane, nuts, spices, ferns, fungus, coloured sand, ice and bread.
- Painstaking hobbies which overtax materials. Handicrafts which ignore the inherent properties of a material.

- Anything made of an inappropriately costly material.
- One material crafted to ape the character of another.
- Shallow material puns.
- Surrogate materials pretending to be more valuable ones, or vice versa.

Design mistakes

- Flat patterns made into 3-D objects, or vice versa.
- Anything made either too heavy or too light.
- Anything with sharp edges; a vessel which does not pour; a handle uncomfortable to hold; anything which cannot be cleaned with ease.
- Combination objects, not optimally suitable for either purpose.
- Functional lies, including architectural ornament.
- Functional objects in forms that have no intelligent relationship to their purpose.
- Machine production that apes the effects of handicraft.
- Frivolous inventions.
- Forgeries.

Decorative mistakes

- Obtrusive or odd proportions.
- Manic ornamentation. Decoration used to disguise flaws.
- Unskilled or unintelligent use of decoration, such as ignoring the natural logic of a botanical motif.
- Surface invasions: marbling wood or paper, gilding porcelain or glass.
- Any decoration created by accident: ink blots, poured glaze, melted wax, pictures drawn in a trance.
- Originality.
- Mockery or misuse of national emblems.
- Anachronisms and exotica.
- Exaggerated finishes including iridescence, fluorescence.
- Primitivism and folk art.

Kitsch mistakes

- Jingoism, souvenirs, folklorica, sportsmen's artefacts, religiosity.

Contemporary mistakes

- Brutalizing objects that encourage aggression.
- Anything made for children.
- Wasted resources, especially single-use or disposable objects.
- Pollution.
- Animal trophies.
- Sexism and racism.
- Exaggerated claims of exclusiveness.

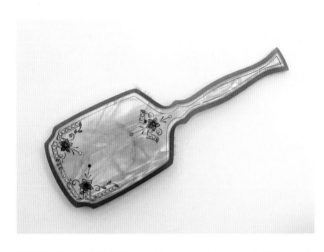

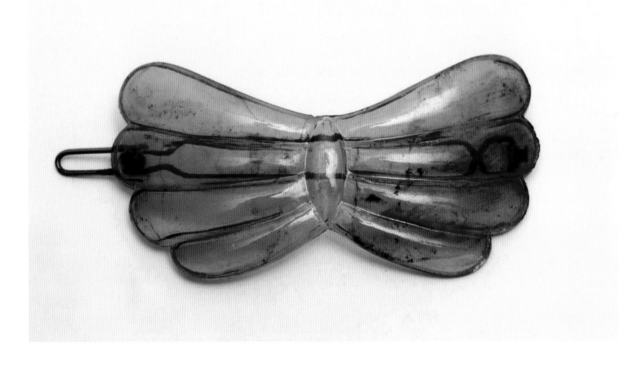

Among all reformers of consumer consciousness and art education, Bauhaus included, Pazaurek's *Principles* have never been surpassed for their detail and thoroughness. Perhaps also for their persuasiveness.

Raw concrete

The matter of raw concrete is a rock-hard case study in the matter of architectural ugliness. Has any material ever been so vilified? Is there a book title more banal than *The History of the Concrete Roofing Tile: Its Origin and Development in Germany* (by Charles Dobson and published by Batsford in London in 1959)? "This book", the blurb carefully explains, "has been compiled with the single aim of interesting those who may like to learn something more about the origin and development of the concrete roofing tile than is generally known in England". Concrete is a certain demonstration that the tropes of Modernism – all those correct and magnificent forms assembled in light – do not always ring true.

Brutalism is now loosely used as a term of denigration, describing the alleged self-conscious ugliness of some – usually concrete – modern architecture. The term was probably coined by Hans Asplund in 1950, although the polymathic architectural historian Reyner Banham popularized it five years later in an article called "The New Brutalism", published in *Architectural Review*, in 1955. (This year was a high noon for intelligent awareness of architecture and design in Britain: in June Ian Nairn had published "Outrage" in the *Architectural Review*, alerting the public, as Henry Cole had a century before, to his fears of a spreading cult of ugliness.) Banham had used Le Corbusier's *béton brut* as a starting point. The French expression simply means "raw concrete". This was a badge of honour for many Modernists, but has come to suggest an aggressive sort of uglification.

Banham was a supporter of the British husband and wife architectural team, Peter and Alison Smithson. The Smithsons built little, but were hugely influential teachers and polemicists in London during the 1950s and '60s. Hard-edged and uncompromising, perhaps even lacking a sense of humour, they had become disenchanted with the way heroic Modernism of the inter-war period had been diluted into either polite Scandiwegian decoration with rugs and stainless platters, or the amusing frivolity of Hugh Casson's Festival of Britain.

Their manifesto was a school they designed in Hunstanton on the North Norfolk coast. When it opened in 1954, it was shockingly original. Materials were exposed and undecorated, the metal structure was made explicit and the mechanical and electrical services were left rhetorically exposed. This is what Banham, perhaps himself a little fatigued by the whimsy and fantasy of Roland Emmett's Far Tottering and Oyster Creek

Opposite Is there a book title more banal than Charles Dobson's *The History of the Concrete Roofing Tile: its origin and development in Germany* (1959)?

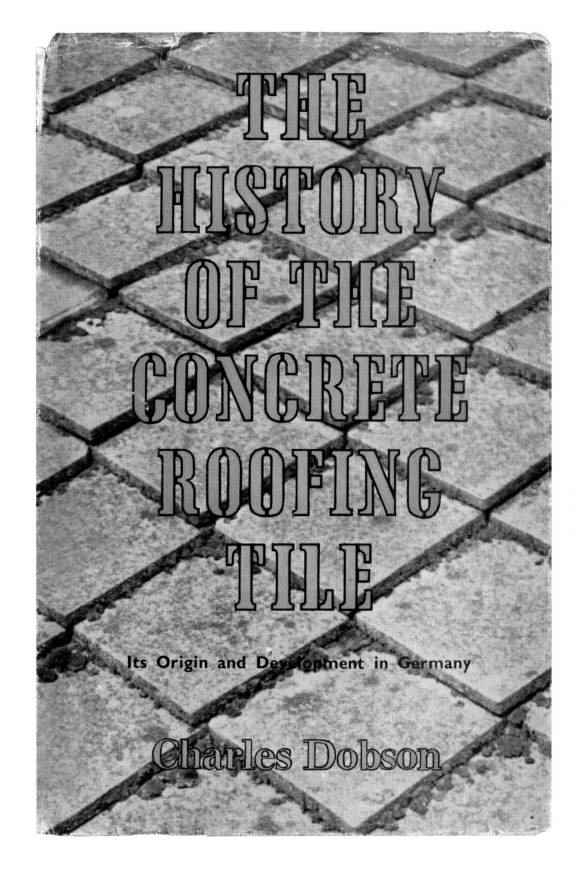

THE HISTORY OF THE CONCRETE ROOFING TILE

Its Origin and Development in Germany

Charles Dobson

SOUTH BANK EXHIBITION

LONDON

1951

FESTIVAL OF BRITAIN

GUIDE PRICE 2/6

Opposite Abram Games's design for the cover of the Festival of Britain catalogue (1951). The Festival was intended to offer a public bruised by war and fatigued by rationing the vision of a polite, Modernist future.

Above Peter and Alison Smithson's Hunstanton Secondary Modern School, Norfolk (1954). The architects were inspired by the pursuit of "ordinariness and light".

Opposite Detail of the Alton Estate, Roehampton (1958–9). The realization of Le Corbusier's 'vertical garden city' in the parkland of south west London. Before this form of social housing became discredited, the Alton Estate was an architects' pilgrimage site.

Overleaf Ernö Goldfinger, Trellick Tower, London (1972), photograph by Mike Seabourne (1999). 'Brutalism' was not originally intended as an insult. When Reyner Banham coined the term it was to describe an architecture that made 'the whole conception of the building plain and comprehensible. No mystery, no romanticism.'

Branch Railway (which appeared in Battersea as a Festival of Britain satellite), called, not without enthusiasm, "The New Brutalism".

He explained that Brutalism intended "to make the whole conception of the building plain and comprehensible. No mystery, no romanticism, no obscurities about function and circulation". Banham admired the way Le Corbusier used *béton brut* as a true sculptural medium. The architect often poured the concrete into rough wooden shuttering, leaving a beautiful impression of (natural) wood grain which was gorgeously tactile in the sunshine of Marseille or the bracing air of the Jura. But when the same technique was applied to social housing at the Alton Estate in Roehampton, or at Park Hill in Sheffield, or Ernö Goldfinger's Trellick Tower in North Kensington or at the Smithsons' own Robin Hood Gardens – it was less successful. Although designed to express "truth", Brutalist buildings were soon condemned as irredeemably ugly.

Interesting, not good

Sometimes they were deemed so even by strict-observation modernists. When Nikolaus Pevsner gave the address at the 1963 opening of Paul Rudolph's School of Architecture at Yale, the audience was scandalied. Pevsner accused Rudolph, an American Brutalist, of departing from Modernism's true path by engaging in dramatic effects. So if truth and beauty have an unclear relationship in twentieth century architecture, so too do ugliness and interest. Le Corbusier's rival in the pantheon of Modernist gods was Mies van der Rohe. Mies once declared, 'I don't want to be interesting, I want to be good.' So yet another distinction was set up in the matter of beauty and ugliness: from natural versus artificial to interesting versus good. Mies, as Paul Goldberger explained in *Building Up and Tearing Down* (2009), was at the centre of the revolution, but he was also a counter-revolutionary who designed beautiful things.

Post-Modernism, a reaction to many things, common sense and Brutalism included, apotheosized "interesting" architecture. Generally, this meant featurism and freakish effects. If a human freak is an example of natural abnormalities, evidence of a deviation from normality into conditions of distress, then Post-Modern architecture and design is its artificial equivalent. If you search for the expression in building design of the dysmorphia found in, say, the Elephant Man, Madame Clofullia, the Bearded Lady of Geneva or Juan Baptista dos Santos (the man with two penises), then consult any encyclopaedia of Post-Modernism. Perhaps significantly, birds are, as in flying ducks, a recurrent motif in the crud of Post-Modern iconography: there were Terry Farrell's bird-like "features" on London's doomed TV-AM building and for Alessi, Michael Graves

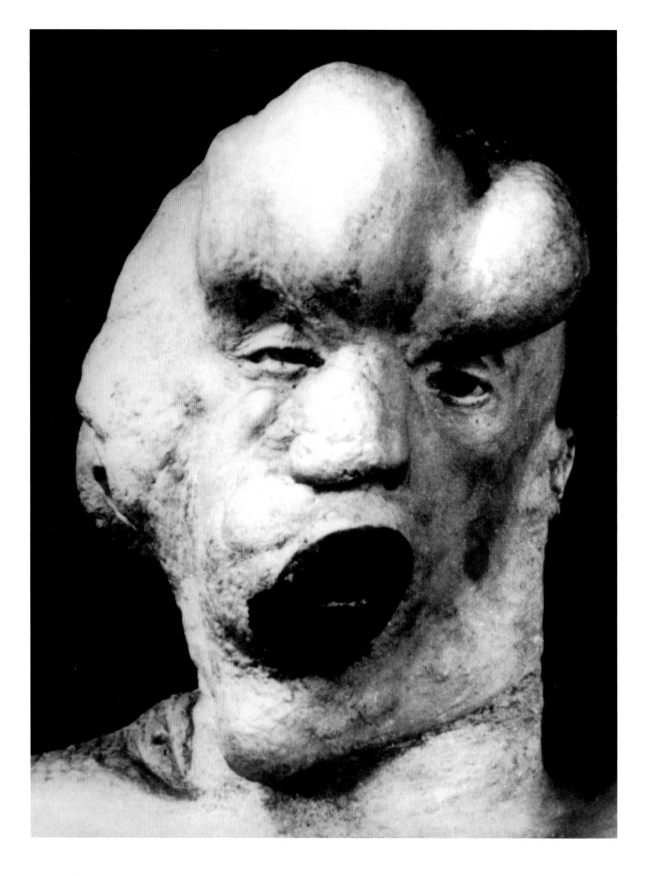

Opposite Joseph Merrick, the "Elephant Man" (c.1880s). Merrick suffered from abnormal skin and bone growth. After he offered himself to a circus, he became something of a celebrity.

Right and overleaf Terry Farrell's TV-am building, London (1983), is essentially a converted garage with amusing egg-cup appendages. Ludicrous animal motifs became a feature of Post-Modern architecture and design in the 80s and 90s. Overleaf left and right: Michael Graves's kettle for Alessi (1985) with a tweety-bird feature and Stefano Giovannoni's *Coccodandy* (1998) basket for cooking eggs, also for Alessi.

designed a *bollitore* with a cute tweety bird. For the same manufacturer, Stefano Giovannoni did a chicken-adorned tool for cooking eggs.

The precise archaeological origins of Post-Modernism are as uncertain as those of Brutalism, although the generalities are indisputable. The holy writ of what became known as Post-Modernism was Robert Venturi's *Complexity and Contradiction in Architecture* (1966). Here was a deliberate attempt to raise the banal to the level of art, to make monuments of kitsch. A complete inversion of Pazaurek's Principles or Adolf Loos's dictums. There is no surer proof of the inconstancy of taste… at least among the artistic elites. There may, however, be an argument that less evolved consumers are more consistent in their preferences.

Venturi worked in a design team with his wife, Denise Scott Brown. Their monument is Guild House in Philadelphia, which, as a retirement home, provided suitably undemanding clients for an architecture which positively aimed to be hokey. Venturi and Scott Brown used ham-fisted details and cheap off-the-shelf components. A fake gold television mast (removed as even psycho-geriatrics found it insulting) stood where an akroterion might have been. This laboured cuteness was typical of the style. And so was the lazy idea that Modernism was only ever favoured because it was cheaper to build than the Neo-classicism it replaced.

The segmentation of ugliness

The architect Gordon Bunshaft of Skidmore Owings & Merrill, who brought Le Corbusier's architectural language to corporate America, said Guild House was 'ugly and ordinary'. This delighted Venturi and Scott Brown who replied 'ugly and ordinary items in culture represent the democratic segment of society, as they embody mass consciousness.' Some, especially in the democratic segment, may have found this patronising. Philip Johnson, who worked with Mies van der Rohe and whose style he enjoyed because it was "easy to copy", called Guild House "ugly and boring". Quite.

Later, Venturi wrote *Learning from Las Vegas*, a hymn to urban sprawl. His praise of uglification was satirized by P. J. O'Rourke:

"As the first Duke of Marlborough did not say when Sir John Vanbrugh presented him with the design for Blenheim Palace, 'It needs a Fotomat booth and a 50-foot-high bank sign giving time, temperature, and interest rates on six-month certificates of deposit. And pave the deer park'".

Even later, Venturi won the competition for the design of the extension to London's National Gallery, a building sponsored by the heir to a supermarket fortune. The magnificent site in Trafalgar Square has historically been associated with skin disorders as commentators struggled and stretched for metaphors to describe eruptions of architectural ugliness. The great architectural historian Henry-Russell Hitchcock, a one-time collaborator with Johnson, damned the silly cupolas on Wilkins's original National Gallery for their morphic similarity to pimples. And Venturi only won the competition after the Prince of Wales in colourful language denounced a serious architectural offering by Ahrends Burton Koralek as a "monstrous carbuncle". So pimples and carbuncles made way for Venturi's ultimate decorated shed. Completed in 1991, in my opinion it is one of the ugliest buildings in all of London.

Robert Venturi, champion of aesthetic squalor, clutter and banality is now more or less ostracized by serious practitioners of and thinkers about architecture.

Above and overleaf Robert Venturi's book *Complexity and Contradiction in Architecture* (1966) was Holy Writ for Post-Modernists. His buildings include Guild House, Philadelphia (1964) and the Sainsbury Wing, National Gallery, London (1982). The Sainsbury building, a dim and lifeless pastiche, replaced a popular design that the Prince of Wales sonorously condemned as a"monstrous carbuncle". Philip Johnson called Guild House "ugly and boring".

We have to be bad

The purity of Modernism represented a dead end, even if the Post-Modernists took a wrong turn in trying to avoid collision with a culminating full-stop. When you have as perfectly refined a product as, say, Dieter Rams' *Schneewittchenssarg* (Snow White's Coffin), there really is nowhere else clean lines can take. Snow White's Coffin was so called not just because of the off-white purity of the metalwork, but because the glass lid resembled the casket in the Disney version of the fairy tale. You could peer into Rams' record player as if looking at the remains of the Bauhaus.

So designers eventually began to look for alternatives. By 1990 the search criteria had been narrowed. This was the year graphic designer Tibor Kalman's speech at the AIGA conference was published in the journal *Print*:

"We have to be bad. Not bad as in crap, but bad as in insubordinate and disobedient. If we're bad, we can be the aesthetic conscience of the business world. We can break the cycle of blandness. We can jam up the assembly line that puts out one dull, lookalike piece of crap after another. We can say 'Why not do something with artistic integrity and ideological courage?' We can say 'Why not do something that forces us to rewrite the definition of 'good design?' Most of all, bad is about recapturing the idea that a designer is the representative – almost like a missionary – of art, within the world of business. We're not here to give them what's safe and expedient. We're not here to eradicate everything of visual interest from the face of the Earth. We're here to make them think about design that's dangerous and unpredictable. We're here to inject art into commerce. We're here to be bad".

This was a favourite text of Patrick le Quément, the car designer who during his tenure as Renault's Chef du Design from 1987–2009, developed a uniquely combative aesthetic. Within a doggedly conservative automobile industry which forever seems to cajole and schmooze its customers with the ersatz elegance of a painted tart, peddling crapola to the credulous, this was brave. Le Quément did not – dare not – use the word "ugly", but he built philosophy out of his intellectually confrontational art. For the first time in the history of consumerism, a major company decided not to seduce customers, but to challenge them.

Le Quément rejected style, dismissing it as "dressing up a hunchback". He wanted to escape the Esperanto that was the universal language of car design. He drew the Renault Vel Satis, routinely considered one of the ugliest cars of modern times. Like the Albert Memorial, it was visibly deformed and used proportions deliberately at odds with known science. It refused to charm. It was *ugga*. And it was, perhaps significantly, a commercial disaster. Beauty may be boring, but consumers do not – at least yet – seem to want its more interesting opposite. Its designer ruefully told me, "You only stumble if you are moving".

History may see the Renault Vel Satis as the end of the process of uglification that began when false principles were established in the world of soot and pistons.

Above SK4 "Snow White's Coffin" radio, Dieter Rams, Braun (1956). Mid-Century Modern or the ultimate homage to numerical control? Rams' design was known as "Snow White's Coffin" because of its transparent lid, but the chilly metaphor has other meanings. With its controlling lines, absolute discipline and near demented restraint, this is the ultimate in classical formalism. You would be astonished to hear noisy, messy music emerging from such a clean machine.

Esquire

MAY 1969
PRICE $1

THE MAGAZINE FOR MEN

**The final decline and total collapse
of the American avant-garde.**

See page 142

10.   Advertising, or Ugliness Sells Badly

Is ugliness a deterrent to success?
Can offence be successful?
Why bother to be tidy?
Is beauty the driver of modern business?

Commercial advertising dare not be ugly. Propaganda is a sort of advertising, and it can most certainly be ugly, indeed, that is often its intention: to persuade and deter through hostility and negativism. But propaganda is only concerned with ideas, not money, changing hands. Advertising, on the other hand, absorbs conventional ideas of beauty and regurgitates them in the service of selling dog food, tampons, holidays and life insurance. See that handsome man at the wheel of a yacht, scouring the horizon? What is he doing? Enjoying the beauty of the seascape? No, he is selling you a Zurich pension.

The exceptions prove the rule. Oliviero Toscani became so fatigued by the visual clichés of lustrous perfection glistening on the cars shown in modern advertising, never scarred by guano or road muck, that he created a radical series of ads for Benetton which did not even show the garments the company was selling. Instead, they showed a blood- and mucus-mired newborn, a bullet-riddled garment, an albino African. Calculated to affront, Toscani's Benetton ads became some of the most celebrated, or, at least, the most discussed, of all time. A primary assumption of advertising, to seduce by beauty, to stimulate desire by perfect form, had been transgressed.

Futurist and Surrealist artists enjoyed an interplay with advertising. Who is to say whether a Horst photograph of a corseted beauty for Vogue in 1934 is an ad or art? It is probably both. And Andy Warhol began his life as an art director in an ad agency. His career thereafter made mass media and gallery art, kitsch and camp indistinguishable from each other. Dismayed, perhaps by the number of Warhol's followers who mistook his irony for career advice, Brian Eno wrote: "The big challenge for artists today is to produce work sufficiently ugly it cannot be appropriated for advertising". Maybe Eno should not have bothered with his concern. Ugliness has now been appropriated by the automobile industry. When this happens, all aesthetic definitions are up for reappraisal.

Renault's Vel Satis was deliberately made hard-to-look-at so as to have stand-out, to use the industry demotic, in a busy marketplace where German *Gute Form* or Italian *bellezza* traditionally dominated morphology. Besides, in making a big car, an area where it had no credentials, Renault could not hope to compete with the successful patrician design language of the German manufacturers. But then a German manufacturer decided to abandon that language.

When the BMW 7 Series was launched in 2001 it was almost universally condemned as "ugly" because of its weird proportions, puckered mouth,

Opposite top/bottom

Benetton campaign for Kosovo humanitarian action, in collaboration with the United Nations High Commission for Refugees, and an invitation to Benetton party (1992). Tired of the conventions of mainstream advertising where everything is shiny, flawless and perfect, the photographer and art director Oliviero Toscani began a series of radical advertisements for Benetton in 1982. They featured alarming images of blood, death and injuries.

squinty eyes, lardy bum, slab sides and deformed aspect. Here was an amorphophallus of the car world. When asked why he had created so obviously a "challenging" shape, BMW's Adrian van Hooydonk replied: "It's very hard to control everybody's perceptions. We always want to do cars which create an emotional response. If you want to avoid all negative criticism, do something boring. I do believe in beauty. And proportion is terribly important to the realization of it. We don't have a rule book. I believe it would limit creativity. But you must not give people what they want. It's *not* a science project".

One central belief of the twentieth century was that beauty could be democratized. So an artificial paradise of industrial perfection could replace the natural paradise of brooks, pastures and forest glades which the very same industry had destroyed. It was a central belief that people wanted beauty. Maybe they did. Maybe they still do. So it is a significant moment in the history of art when Adrian van Hooydonk, one of the most influential designers in the world, says he wants to withhold the beauty which his consumers are assumed to crave.

When beauty was democratized, it became a bicycle

Whether in the breach or the observance, Karl Marx, in either way, continues best to represent the arguments about the perplexing relationships of art, industry and nature. Marx also fretted about whether being determines consciousness or whether consciousness determines being: do we make our fate or does fate make us? To this end it is worth recording that Marx' own being was most unfortunately covered in ugly boils and carbuncles. To what extent this uncomfortable disfigurement soured his view of the world and its consumers we cannot say, but his observation – (made in the *Economic and Philosophic Manuscripts* of 1844) that while a rich man may be ugly, he can be redeemed by acquiring beauty – is a perfect gloss on consumerism. Perhaps Marx yearned for aesthetic redemption through the acquisition of perfect dry goods.

The mythology of Modernism depends on the idea that, if industry follows certain rules laid down by "designers", beauty will be the result. Modernism could remake the world. To this majestic belief there have been many objectors. Proust, an exquisite, found it perverse that anyone could see beauty in, for example, a banal railway carriage. When we have already seen Siena, Venice and Granada, Proust wonders how a train could possibly advance beauty's cause. Perhaps inspired by a line of passing carriages, he says that beauty is a "sequence of hypotheses which ugliness cuts short". It is an anticipation of pleasure. However he does allow that military aircraft seen at night can be beautiful as is the sound of "that little insect throbbing up there". Proust, of course, had never had his fundament shaken by a B-52.

Proust also has many, generally positive, observations on bicycles. Can a bicycle, that most elementary, but perfect, example of industrial production be beautiful? The hysterical Ouida thought not. Apart from anything else: "No man or woman with the slightest aesthetic sense could assume the ludicrous position necessary for it". She may have recently read Lord Chesterfield's splendid comment on erotic love: "the pleasure is momentary, the position ridiculous and the expense damnable".

But the great fear was what the bicycle might do to manners. Like Ruskin, Ouida thought institutionalized sport sullied the natural world. Ruskin worried that his beloved Alps were becoming racetracks while Ouida was particularly moved by the aesthetic horrors of competitive cycling. To a certain nineteenth century psychology, sport was not an entertainment, but a spectre of revolutionary destruction: "Behold him in the velodrome as he yells insanely after his kind as they tear along on their tandem machines in a match, and then ask yourself candidly, O my reader, if any age before this… ever produced any creature so utterly low and loathsome, so physically, mentally, individually and collectively hideous… making life and death and all eternity seem ridiculous by the mere existence of his own intolerable fatuity and bestiality".

Despite these objections – "the beauty of the earth is dying," Ouida moaned – the bicycle ceased to be construed as an ugly contraption and became a source of aesthetic delight, an exemplar of modern possibilities. The design of the bicycle was in all essentials established well over a century ago. There have been continuous improvements in materials technology and componentry, while the subtleties of frame geometry continue – via debate – to evolve, but here is a rare example of a concept so nearly perfect that radical change will never occur. The bicycle will develop, but so long as humans have legs and a requirement to shift their carcasses beyond easy walking range, the bicycle, it seems, will remain.

Although there are many contenders for the claim, John Kemp Starley (1854–1901) is usually credited with the final definition of the "safety bicycle". This was during the 1880s, a turbulent and competitive moment among the bicycle designer-entrepreneurs who were one of the most exciting and distinctive products of Victorian capitalism. It was not immediately obvious that the Starley two-wheel design was inevitable: there were, for example, many advocates of tricycles. But as the old, asymmetric, treacherous, high-mounted "Ordinary" (or Penny-Farthing) became less and less acceptable from a health and safety point of view, the design options became helpfully limited.

Notwithstanding Ouida's horror at the velodrome, the experience of using a bicycle was both socially audacious and physically exhilarating, when not actually dangerous. In an essay called "Taming the Bicycle",

STARLEY & SUTTON,

Meteor Works, West Orchard,

COVENTRY.

"The 'Rover' has set the fashion to the world."—*Cyclist.*

18½ MILES IN THE HOUR; 30½ MILES IN 1 hr. 41 min. ON THE HIGH ROAD.

The "Rover," as ridden by Lord BURY, President N.C.U.

MANUFACTURERS OF THE CELEBRATED

"ROVER" BICYCLE,

THE "ROAMER" & OTHER TRICYCLES,

"COVENTRY CHAIR," &c., &c.

Price Lists and Testimonials Free.　　Full Illustrated Catalogue, 2 Stamps.

Au Palais-Sport.

Mark Twain described progress as a "weaving, tottering" sequence of accidents avoided. To address the shortcomings, by 1885 Starley had settled on a successful general arrangement: his Rover had a low mount, wheels of 36 inches in diameter in the front, 30 in the rear, triangular frame, chain drive to the rear. His brief to himself was to create "the right position in relation to the pedals" at "the proper distance from the ground".

In September of that year George Smith covered 100 miles on a Rover in seven hours and five minutes. Consumerized improvements followed, a sprung seat, for example, but a timeless classic had been established. In the late 1890s, Starley's business was renamed The Rover Cycle Company, ancestor of the ill-fated car company. Some see it as elegiac that a British classic evolved into a British catastrophe.

Because the bicycle was such a perfect expression of the machine aesthetic (and, perhaps, the best proof of the form-follows-function argument), it was soon adopted as a symbol by the early Modernist architects and designers. In 1910 Joseph August Lux, a member of the Deutscher Werkbund, declared 'a bicycle is beautiful' because it was an explicit diagram of forces. This polemic fed directly into the philosophy of the Bauhaus. Indeed, the famous "Bauhaus" chair designed by Marcel

Breuer was of a tubular steel construction said to be inspired by a bicycle's handlebars. Certainly, the perception of a bicycle as beautiful, as opposed to a rude product of industry, is an idea that would have interested Lewis Carroll.

Chutzpah, chrome and Eau de Cologne

The belief that technology refined by art could create democratized beauty was one of the great persuasive myths of twentieth century design. With the perspective of the twenty-first century we can, however, now see that the idea of "design" itself was also itself a persuasive myth. And like all mythologies, it threw up some god-like figures whose job was to sustain the belief system. The idea of the designer as a shaman, as a wizard – perhaps even a divine consultant – who can create beauty where hitherto there had only been mess and squalor – had no better champion than Raymond Loewy. A French émigré once described as an inch deep and a mile wide, Loewy can serve as a perfect exemplar of modern witchcraft. He cast spells on ugliness, turned ugly ducklings into swans.

In the middle of a startling and very well-publicised career of charlatan-like legerdemain, repairing the ugly products of industry by dressing them with his own thoughts, Loewy wrote a very good book. Or perhaps had a very good book written for him. *Never Leave Well Enough Alone* was published in New York in 1951. When an edition appeared in his native French, it was retitled *La laideur se vend mal*, but the theme was essentially the same. With chutzpah, chrome, Eau de Cologne and a gaudy sense of style, Loewy turned ugly industrial products into soothing beautiful ones. He told his blinking clients that the most beautiful thing in the world was a rising sales chart.

He translated the awkward and the banal into the elegant and fetching. He even described the early days of the Machine Age as "messy dirty noisy bulky". These ugly features could, by his improving genius, be eliminated. Design was the avenging angel, remedying ills. *Never Leave Well Enough Alone* has a series of transformations from ugly to beautiful: the Gestetner duplicator, the Coldspot fridge, Flexvac vacuum seal packing machines, Coke dispensers, the International Harvester cream separator, the Cummins cheque-perforating machine, the Singer vacuum cleaner and Mobil car battery.

So here was the remedial power of design to turn ugly mistakes into beautiful purpose. This was the alchemy of design! To beautify! To tidy up! To exclude dirt! And, by the way, to sell. With his redesign of the Lucky Strike cigarette packaging and advertising in 1940, Raymond Loewy even made fags a thing of beauty. Loewy was the absolute paradigm of the "designer" as an agent representing beauty in the battle against ugliness.

VOL. LIX. No. 1512.   PUCK BUILDING, New York, February 21, 1906.   PRICE TEN CENTS.

"What Fools these Mortals be!"

Puck

Copyright, 1906, by Keppler & Schwarzmann.

Entered at N. Y. P. O. as Second-class Mail Matter.

THE UGLY DUCKLING.

The Senate is indignant over the attacks on it in American magazines.   A suggestion under consideration is that some able expounder be selected to deliver a response to the criticisms. — *Daily Press.*

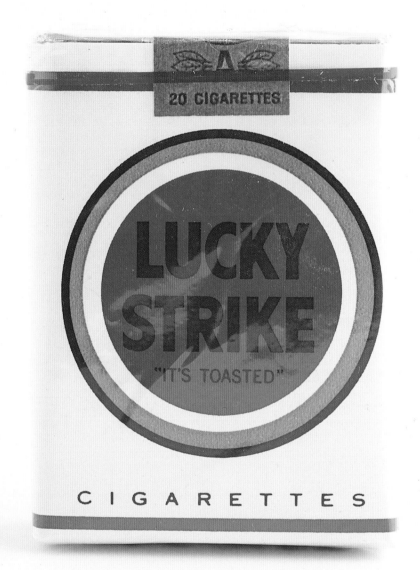

After the Second World War in Germany, Dieter Rams performed similar transformations on brown boxes of electrical goods and turned them first into white, then into black boxes.

It was persuasive, but Rams left no great book behind. In contrast, Loewy's *Never Leave Well Enough Alone* is perhaps one of the greatest business books of the twentieth century. An even greater one was Frederick Winslow Taylor's *The Principles of Scientific Management* (1911). This was the source of "Taylorism" the time-and-motion studies which established the beat of American industrial production which Raymond Loewy beautified. With his clipboard and stopwatch Taylor invigilated messy, sloppy humans to make them more like machines. Again, it was persuasive for a while, but we now know that Taylor falsified his data. Rather in the same way, Raymond Loewy falsified his arguments. (And it need hardly be added that many of Loewy's claims that his version of beauty brought commercial advantage by satisfying a nation's avid consuming aesthetes were, to put it no higher, exaggerated. Many of Loewy's designs were commercial flops.)

Artists no longer use the term "beauty". Does that mean it no longer exists? Or have we just given up the chase? Certainly, the standards by which beauty might be measured are so elusive it is tempting to suggest they might never be captured. Ugliness has its champions: today the architect Rem Koolhaas finds ugliness more interesting than beauty, without ever troubling to define either. Although the disturbing Dutch architect's interest in ugliness is consistent: he once told the critic Edwin Heathcote that in restaurants he likes to order "ugly food".

Here, perhaps, is a link between the ideas of function which underwrite architecture and the ideas of nutrition which underwrite cooking. Building and cooking also have a visual character. Each is united by ideas about taste and display. And architecture is, in general, now a form of brand management or popular entertainment. Writing of the Westin Hotel on New York's Times Square, a design by the flamboyant Miami firm Arquitectonica, *The New Yorker*'s architecture critic Paul Goldberger said, "It is not easy nowadays to go beyond the bounds of taste". But that, it seems, for many artists, architects and designers is exactly the challenge they have set themselves.

Anyway, Proust thought ugliness aristocratic because it suggests a confidence about not having to please anyone. And "ugliness is superior to beauty because it lasts longer", according to grizzled chanteur Serge Gainsbourg. Peter Schjeldahl, *The New Yorker*'s art critic summed up the hiatus nicely: "Beauty is, or ought to be, no big deal, but the lack of it is".

Ugliness really is a big deal. But, then, if everything were beautiful… nothing would be.

Index

Selected Bibliography

Is it surprising that the literature of ugliness is rather thin and mean? A subject with pre-historic credentials and Biblical resonance, essential to an understanding of Darwinian evolution as well as capitalist commerce, not to mention romantic love, sex, pornography, advertising, art, architecture and industrial design, has attracted very, very few commentators.

No attempt has been made in this bibliography to include all the sources consulted or cited. Indeed, very few of the books listed here have any substantial treatment of ugliness, but they all touch upon – or in Kant's case sit very heavily upon – ideas of attraction and repulsion which helped my understanding of this slippery subject. Each provides an important and interesting extension of ideas included in this book.

Adorno, T., *Ästhetische Theorie*, Suhrkamp Verlag, Frankfurt 1970.
A posthumous collection of the daunting thinker's 1960s essays. The original was dedicated to absurdist Irish playwright Samuel Beckett. The 1997 English edition copied the original's aggressive conceit of printing an unbroken text without paragraphs.

Bayley, S., *Taste – the secret meaning of things*, Faber and Faber, London 1991.
A recklessly synoptic account of a treacherous subject.

Boyd, R., *The Australian Ugliness*, F. W. Cheshire, Melbourne 1960.
A brilliant critique of Australian townscape by a fearless native: a rare example of a book in English, or indeed, any language with the word "ugliness" in its title. Boyd has great fun condemning the Australian architect's resort to "featurism" in pursuit of visual interest.

Burke, E., *A Philosophical Enquiry into the Origin of the Sublime and the Beautiful*, R. and J. Dodsley, London 1756.
A gazetteer balanced between Romantic symbolism and rational analysis. Burke considers the visual sources of distress and delight; at one point, he discusses what would later become known as "functionalism".

Cronin, V., *The Golden Honeycomb*, Rupert Hart-Davis, London 1954.
An elegant Sicilian travel book with some beautiful accounts of the confrontational nature of the island's extreme baroque architecture.

Darwin, C., *The Expression of Emotion in Man and Animals*, John Murray, London 1872.
Published thirteen years after his epochal *On the Origin of Species*, this analysis of facial expression, researched using photographs, was the beginning of modern behavioural science.

Dorfles, G., *Kitsch: the World of Bad Taste*, Gabriele Mazzotta, Milan 1968.
This account of Kitsch by the Milanese polymath has never been surpassed in wit, scope and pertinence.

Eco, U., *On Ugliness*, Rizzoli, New York 2007.
Originally published as *Storia della Bruttezza*, a title which plays on the Italian idea of 'bella figura'. Eco curates a fabulous literary and visual anthology, but he rarely deals with ugliness, more often with grotesques and kitsch. These are not quite the same thing.

Gombrich, E. H., 'Leonardo's Method of Analysis and Permutation: the Grotesque Heads", lecture, 1952, reprinted in *The Heritage of Apelles: Studies in the Art of the Renaissance*, p57-75, Cornell University Press, Ithaca (N. Y.), 1976.
The world's most successful art historian considers why Leonardo found ugliness as fascinating as beauty.

Greenberg, C., "Avant-Garde and Kitsch", The Partisan Review fall issue, p34-49, Boston (MA), 1939.
The great, conservative New York art critic introduced the word "kitsch" to the English language.

Hardy, G. H., *A Mathematician's Apology*, Cambridge University Press, Cambridge 1940.
Mathematicians often call equations and solutions 'beautiful'. In this memoir Hardy digresses on different sources of attraction and repulsion.

Hayden, D. B., *Seven American Utopias: the architecture of communitarian socialism 1790-1975*, MIT Press, Cambridge (MA) 1976.
An encyclopedic and scholarly study of American communities, many of which made a cult of austere 'beauty'.

Kant, E., *Kritik der reinen Vernunft*, Johann Friedrich Hartknoch, Riga 1781.
The *Critique of Pure Reason* considers how the different senses cope with disgusting stimuli. I have not read this and nor have I ever met anyone who has, but it would be perverse not to include it. Its baffling nature has inspired slews of articles on 'why Kant finds nothing ugly'.

Le Corbusier, *The Modulor*, English ed.: Faber and Faber, 1958.
The great Swiss-French architect's proprietary system of proportion. Building design, Corb insisted, should be based on the human body. Beauty will result.

Lehman-Haupt, H., *Art Under a Dictatorship*, Oxford University Press, New York (N. Y.), 1954.
Detailed analyses of how totalitarian politicians, especially Nazis, have an apparently inexorable inclination to sponsor kitsch.

Loewy, R., *Never Leave Well Enough Alone*, Simon and Schuster, New York (N.Y.) 1951.
A stylish, if smugly overbearing, apologia by one of the pioneers of consultant design. Beauty drives desire, Loewy believed. The French edition was called *La Laideur Se Vend Mal*.

Mobius, M. M., & Rosenblat, T.S., "Why Beauty Matters", *American Economic Review* 96, NO.1: p222-235, 2006.
An evidence-based attempt to quantify the competitive advantage of "beauty".

Olalquiaga, C., *The Artificial Kingdom – a treasury of the kitsch experience*, Pantheon, New York (N.Y.) 1998.
> A dense, rich, strange book that is particularly good on the curiosities of High Victorian taste.

Pacioli, L., *De divina prorportione*, Venice 1509.
> The original manuscript is in Milan's Biblioteca Ambrosiana. Pacioli, who also established the methodology of modern accounting, developed theories about correct proportion that were influential on many Italian artists.

Pazaurek, G. E., *Geschmacksverirrungen im Kunstgewerbe*, Stuttgart 1919.
> A comprehensive, hilarious, and still relevant account of design mistakes and their consequences by the director of Stuttgart's Arts and Crafts Museum. An occult influence on the entire modernist sensibility.

Plato, *The Republic*, c. 380BC.
> The original was known as *Politeia*. Innumerable modern editions have made it, quite literally, the *locus classicus* of any discussion about perfect – and imperfect - form.

Ramachandran, V.S., "The Science of Art: a neurological theory of aesthetic experience", *The Journal of Consciousness Studies* 6: p6-7, 1999.
> An attempt by a leading researcher in the emerging discipline of neuroaesthetics to explain art in terms of laboratory science.

Ramé, M. L. (Ouida), "The Ugliness of Modern Life", *The Nineteenth Century*: vol. XXXIX, 1896.
> Ouida was a hyperactive, conservative and possibly hysterical Victorian novelist who wrote: "Familiarity is a magician that is cruel to beauty but kind to ugliness".

Renner, H. D., *The Origin of Food Habits*, Faber and Faber, London 1944.
> A study published in the context of wartime discussion of diet and nutrition, Renner includes diverting anecdotal material about the variations of taste in different cultures.

Rosenkranz, K., *Ästhetik des Häßlichen*, Gebrüder Borntraeger, Berlin 1853.
> The very first book to treat ugliness. Rosenkranz was an academic philosopher of the Hegelian school. I have never been able to find, still less read, a copy.

Ruskin, J., *The Two Paths*, Smith, Elder & Co., London 1859.
> Five lectures by the radical-conservative who railed against the ruinous changes which industrialization brought to the English town and country. The polemical equivalent of Lewis Carroll's "uglification".

Shelley, M., *Frankenstein; or, the Modern Prometheus*, Lackington, Hughes, Harding, Mavor, & Jones, London 1818.
> The ultimate horror story, with its hideous monster, can be read as a gloss on the alarm Shelley's contemporaries felt about the intrusion science and industry were making into hitherto unspoilt Nature.

Sprigg, J. & Larkin, D., *Shaker: Life, Work and Art*, Houghton Mifflin, Wilmington (MA) 1991.
> A masterly survey of the architecture and design of the ascetic New England community whose founding mother was driven across the Atlantic by disgust at her native Manchester. The Shakers insisted that their version of beauty was divine.

Stern, J. & Stern, M., *The Encyclopedia of Bad Taste*, HarperCollins, Scranton (PA) 1990.
> A vulgarian masterpiece, with appropriately shocking and hilarious illustrations.

Synott, A., *The Body Social – Symbolism, Self and Society*. Routledge, Florence (KY) 1993.
> A sociologist considers how notions of attractiveness influence human behaviour.

Zeki, S., *Inner Vision: an exploration of Art and the Brain*, Oxford University Press, New York (NY) 1999.
> The leading neuroaesthetician's boldest attempt to quantify what he later called "the neural correlates of beauty".

Picture credits

The publishers would like to thank the following sources for their
kind permission to reproduce the pictures in this book.

Alamy/Art Archive: 107
Allen Ginsberg Estate: 76
Arcaid: 239, 240, 241
Bridgeman Art Library: Sir Edward Coley Burne-Jones/Birmingham Museums & Art Gallery: 176–177,
Vatican Museums and Galleries, Vatican City: 12, Museum of Fine Arts, Houston, Texas: 100,
Charles Darwin, *The Expression of the Emotions in Man and Animals,* **John Murray, 1872:** 16, 19
Creative Commons: 26, 36, 41, 82, 84–85, 146, 147, 154 (left), 184, 189, Acquired by Henry Walters with
the Massarenti Collection, 1902: 61, Library of Parliament, Cape Town: 124, Smallbones: 243, Amanda
Vincent-Rous: 234
Corbis: 67, Andreas Gursky/Albright-Knox Art Gallery: 102–103, & Art Archive: 104, Bettmann: 139
(bottom), Brooklyn Museum: 160, The Gallery Collection: 20, 88, Peter Harholdt: 129, Historical Picture
Archive: 92–93, Hulton-Deutsch Collection: 139 (top), Richard Klune: 191, David Lees: 40, Francis G. Mayer:
87, Mediscan: 66, Gideon Mendel: 213, Bo Zaunders: 262
© David Moratilla: 11
Fiell Image Archive: 31, 34–35, 56, 59, 65, 67, 68l, 73, 112, 113, 116, 117, 121, 126, 131, 132, 133, 134, 144,
148–149, 151, 152–153, 154 (right), 155, 156, 159, 178, 182–183, 186–187, 190, 196–197, 199, 200, 204, 224,
226, 231, 232, 257, 260, 263, photographs by Paul Chave: 27, 140, 154 (right), 155, 244–245, 272
© FUEL/Danzig Baldaev: 207
Getty Images: 3, 28–29, 39, 48–49, 62, 79, 96, 123, 137, 142–143, 202, 203, 211, 219, AFP: 138 (bottom), 220,
223, 251 (top), Jean-Etienne Liotard/Bridgeman Art Library: 108, Peter Dazeley: 150, Gamma-Keystone: 208–
209, Gamma-Rapho: 251 (bottom), Michael Ochs Archives: 75, Popperfoto: 138 (top), Time & Life Pictures:
4–5, 69 (right), 111, UIG: 52
iStockphoto.com: 2, 42–43, 50, 120, 166
Library of Congress Prints & Photographs Division, Washington DC: 32, 80–81, 98, 135, 136, 259
Mary Holland: /http://www.naturallycuriouswithmaryholland.wordpress.com: 118
Collection of Werkbundarchiv/Museum der Dinge: photographs by Armin Herrmann: 228–229
Nature Picture Library: Doug Wechsler: 125, Xi Zhinong: 55
Photo courtesy of Wright: 247
Photo Scala, Florence: 14–15, courtesy of the Ministero Beni e Att. Culturali: 21, 89, 114–115, 248, Ann
Ronan/Heritage Images: 24–25, Museum of Modern Art, New York: 216, National Portrait Gallery: 63
Photoshot: 70–71
Picture-Desk: Private Collection/Marc Charmet/Art Archive: 45, Musée des Arts Décoratifs Paris/Collection
Dagli Orti /Art Archive: 213, Museum of London: 236–237, Kharbine-Tapabor/Art Archive: 198
Rex Features: Everett Collection: 195
RIBA Library Photographs Collection: John Maitby: 233
Richard Sexton: 46–47
Science & Society Picture Library: 22, 23, 91, 95, 97, 119, 173, 174–175, 255, 256, National Railway Museum:
171–172
Thinkstockphotos.co.uk: 6, 162–163, 165, 169, 252
Topfoto.co.uk: 238, IMAGNO/Franz Hubmann: 220
Wellcome Library: 192

Every effort has been made to acknowledge correctly and contact the source and/or copyright holder of each
picture and Carlton Books Limited apologises for any unintentional errors or omissions, which will be corrected
in future editions of this book.

Acknowledgements

Here's a question: who'd want to be acknowledged as a help and inspiration in a book about ugliness? While every timid person stands back, I can name-check a few bold individuals. This, obviously, is not an academic study. It's more of what Peter Mandelson, attempting to remedy the lies and distortions of the 1997 New Labour manifesto, called a 'suggestive essay.' As in all things everywhere and all the time, my constant (but not at all complacent) companion Flo has been influential. Many of the ideas printed here have been tested on her in the kitchen. Most of them failed. Then there is a historic debt. This is Dr 'Jimmy' Quentin Hughes, my late mentor and one of the most stylish figures I have ever met. A brave soldier and mischievous conversationalist, he was presiding genius at Liverpool School of Architecture and a lifelong supporter of the bar at the Philharmonic Dining Rooms. I owe him a lot, especially memories of conversations about this very subject while I sat, awestruck, in one of the very few Eames chairs in North West England. Formal sources have been no help, but a lot of what is in this book is the product of many agreeable conversations with witty, combative friends: John Gordon, Michael Hoppen, and Adam Zamoyski, for example. Many thanks to Peter Dawson and Louise Evans of Grade Design for their hard work on the superb design of this book. And finally, of course, the confident and generous people of Goodman Fiell, especially Peter and Charlotte Fiell, and project editor Isabel Wilkinson. I am very grateful they have made such a beautiful job of such an ugly subject.